Visualizing Isaiah

DONALD W. PARRY

Frontispiece: The sun rises over Sinai.

Right, from top: Camels in the Sinai desert, a spring of water near Tel Dan, an acacia tree, fish at the market, a rustic plow.

The Foundation for Ancient Research and Mormon Studies (FARMS)
Institute for the Study and Preservation of Ancient Religious Texts,
Brigham Young University
P.O. Box 7113
University Station
Provo, Utah 84602

Library of Congress Cataloging-in-Publication Data

Parry, Donald W.
Visualizing Isaiah / Donald W. Parry.
p. cm.
Includes bibliographical references and index.
ISBN 0-934893-58-6 (alk. paper)
1. Bible. O.T. Isaiah—Commentaries. I. Title.
BS1515.3 .P375 2001
224'.1077—dc21

2001003392

CONTENTS

ACKNOWLEDGMENTS

I extend appreciation to all whose efforts have made this book possible. In particular, I thank Tana and Mac Graham, for traveling to the Holy Land with the express purpose of taking photographs for this volume; Sunny Larson, for editing the manuscript and coordinating the efforts of those involved in the volume's layout, editing, and publication; Carmen Cole, for photo editing, interior and cover design; Bjorn Pendleton, for interior design; Alison Coutts, for overall coordination and support; Carrilyn Clarkson, for photography, photo editing, and image consultation; Jay A. Parry and Tina M. Peterson, my coauthors on *Understanding Isaiah* (Deseret Book, 1998), for permitting me to adapt parts of that volume for *Visualizing Isaiah;* D. Kelly Ogden, for his careful review of the manuscript, especially the maps; Mindy Anderson, S. Kent Brown, Justin Craig, Arnold H. Green, Matthew J. Grey, Leigh Gunnell, Brent Hall, Andy North, D. Kelly Ogden, John W. Welch, for photography; Laren R Robison, for his expertise on plants and animals; Andrew Livingston, for cover design and maps; and Julie Dozier, for copyrights and permissions.

Donald W. Parry

Left: Remains of Robinson's Arch, at the southwestern corner of Jerusalem's Temple Mount. The lower stones belong to the period of Herod the Great.

INTRODUCTION

Isaiah and Symbolism—Reading the Silence

My colleague, J. Scott Miller, a professor of Japanese at Brigham Young University, related the following story:

> Immediately after graduating from BYU I spent some time as a graduate research fellow at a Japanese university. During that time I inherited an advisor who . . . had great interests in philosophy and music (he had a grand piano in his tiny office, around which we would conduct our conversations). One day we were discussing the concept of space when he suddenly played a first, then a second note on the piano.
>
> "What do you hear?" he asked.
>
> "A fifth," I replied.
>
> "No, what are you *listening* to?" he inquired more earnestly, playing the notes again.
>
> "Two notes," I responded, puzzled.
>
> "That is precisely the point. You hear the notes. We Japanese hear the silence in between. Westerners focus on what is *there,* Asians focus on what is *not.*" (*Maeser's Edge,* 12/6:1, emphasis in original)

Many of us read Isaiah's words like Westerners hear musical notes. We grasp the literal sense of the language but fail to perceive the *imagery* behind the words. We are fully aware of the obvious—the two notes of music—but unaware of what exists beyond the apparent. For example, some read "cedars of Lebanon" and "oaks of Bashan" (Isaiah 2:12–13) and see only trees in their mind's eye. They do not recognize the symbolism of tall cedars and oaks representing proud people. Or some read "idols of gold" (Isaiah 2:20) and see only man-made statues. They do not realize that idols may signify any kind of false worship.

The book of Isaiah cannot be read like a newspaper, a letter, or a textbook. Symbolism is a key element of Isaiah's text. It is part of every chapter and almost every verse. Through revelation, Isaiah drew upon the social, cultural, religious, and political background of the day to produce hundreds of different symbols. His symbols pertain to various aspects of life in the Holy Land: he wrote of the natural world, including animals, insects, plants, rocks, elements, and objects in the sky; he mentioned colors, numbers, foods, armor, and weaponry; he referred to persons, occupations, ecclesiastical offices, social relationships, and human anatomy; and he wrote of places and architecture.

This volume is not a scholarly work but is designed as an introduction to Isaiah for readers of all ages—families, students, teachers. Children can gain entry into the world of Isaiah through the pictures, and youth and adults through both commentary and

Right: A stand of cedars of Lebanon, east of Byblos, Lebanon.

pictures. The "How to Use This Book" section that follows describes how this book is organized.

It is hoped that the photographs, illustrations, and maps will enable readers of all ages to more easily visualize many of Isaiah's teachings and prophecies. The photograph of a pruning hook (page 118) serves as an example. The pruning hook is a metal, knifelike instrument with a short, broad blade attached to a wooden handle. It is used for pruning vines and harvesting grapes. The pruning hook is similar to a spearhead, which also has a short, broad blade attached to a wooden handle. After viewing the photograph of the pruning hook, one can more easily comprehend how a spearhead can be beaten with a hammer and reshaped into a pruning hook. Isaiah's prophecy, "They shall beat their swords into plowshares, and their spears into pruninghooks" (Isaiah 2:4) takes on new meaning.

All but two or three of the photographs presented in this book were taken in the Holy Land. It seemed proper that the photos originate from Isaiah's homeland and surrounding regions. Though much has changed in the Holy Land since Isaiah prophesied and ministered more than 2,700 years ago, a great deal remains the same. Shepherds gather their sheep into sheepfolds; grass grows on the rooftops of some dwellings; farmers use beasts of burden to plow their fields; olive trees grow throughout the Judean hills; donkeys pull carts loaded with goods; ancient watchtowers rise into the sky; Bedouin pitch their tents and ride camels; and the cities of Jerusalem, Damascus, and Bethlehem remain. The wilderness of Judea, the Sea of Galilee, and other prominent geographical features of the Holy Land have changed little since Isaiah's time, and the same is fundamentally true of the Holy Land's plants and animals. The photographs, taken in the Holy Land, attempt to capture as closely as possible the world Isaiah experienced during his ministry and drew upon as he wrote. If a person knows no more about Isaiah than what is presented here, he or she will have a good basic overview of some of the main religious concepts.

Below: Sheep near Bethphage. A black sheep, upper left, strays from the flock.

HOW TO USE THIS BOOK

This book is composed of verses from Isaiah accompanied by commentary, pictures, captions, charts, and maps. Each of the parts is designed to give the reader further understanding of Isaiah and his world.

Selected Verses from Isaiah

The verses cited in this volume, unless otherwise noted, are from the King James Version of the Bible. The subject matter of the verses is illuminated by the commentary, pictures, and captions.

Commentary

The commentary, located immediately below the verses, consists of brief explanations and observations about the verses. The commentary, of course, does not represent the final word on any given matter, nor is it the only valid explanation. It is based on the author's opinion and an understanding of the scriptures from the point of view of a member of the Church of Jesus Christ of Latter-day Saints. For complete context, full notes, comments, and bibliographic sources, see the author's *Understanding Isaiah* as well as other books listed in the "Sources Consulted" section.

Pictures

One or more pictures accompany the verses from Isaiah. The pictures relate to specific words in the verses. For example, the picture of the Salt Lake Temple accompanies the verse about the "Lord's house" being "established in the top of the mountains," and the picture of the sand dunes near Gaza illustrates the "sand of the sea."

Captions

These are placed next to the pictures. The captions provide details, often of cultural significance, about the pictures.

Charts

These are not directly related to the commentary, pictures, or captions; rather, they address ideas and events found throughout the book of Isaiah. They add information about Isaiah, his writings, or the world from which he came.

Maps

Isaiah's book refers to more than one hundred different places, cities, and countries, such as Jerusalem, Damascus, Lebanon, Bashan, Assyria, Egypt, Moab, and Edom. The maps were made expressly for this volume to give the reader a location for the places mentioned in Isaiah's writings. The maps are placed throughout the volume, correlating with general sections of the book and not with specific pictures and commentary on a particular page.

Sources Consulted

To make this volume easier to use and accessible to a wide range of readers, there are very few in-text citations. For those interested in documentation or more information on topics discussed in this volume, the bibliography offers several helpful sources.

A view of Wadi Qelt, the Judean desert.

ANCIENT ISRAEL

In Isaiah's time, the Holy Land consisted of two kingdoms, the southern kingdom of Judah and the northern kingdom of Israel. Isaiah prophesied to his contemporaries in Jerusalem and other cities and villages in both kingdoms. He spoke against idolatrous practices, social injustices, and pride. He gave members of the kingdoms instructions on caring for the poor, widows, and fatherless. He invited them to repent and cleanse themselves through the power of the atonement. And he taught them the way to happiness and peace.

The vision of Isaiah the son of Amoz, which he saw concerning Judah and Jerusalem in the days of Uzziah, Jotham, Ahaz, and Hezekiah, kings of Judah.

World Timeline of the Century When Isaiah Lived, 800–700 B.C.

ca. 800	Etruscans settle in Italy
ca. 780	Hosea and Amos begin their ministries
776	First Olympic games take place in Olympia, Greece
775	First authenticated date in Chinese history (because of solar eclipse)
772	At Ephesus, construction begins on the Temple of Artemis, one of the seven wonders of the world
771	China's Chou capital at Hao destroyed by northern Jung barbarians
ca. 767	Uzziah becomes king of Judah at age sixteen
753	According to tradition, Rome is founded by Romulus and Remus
750	King of Nubia conquers Egypt
750	The Marib Dam, Yemen, is built, lasting almost 1000 years
750	Celts reach Britain
740	Homer, author of *The Iliad* and *The Odyssey,* lives
740	Isaiah begins his ministry
ca. 739	Jotham becomes king of Judah
ca. 734	Ahaz becomes king of Judah
ca. 728	Hezekiah becomes king of Judah
722	First entry in the *Annals of Lu,* Chinese historical records
722–1	Assyrians conquer northern kingdom of Israel, take away the ten tribes
722	The prophet Micah's ministry
710	Hezekiah institutes religious reforms
708	Empire of Medes established by Deioces
705	Hesiod, Greek poet, authors "Theogony"
701	Babylonians make advances in understanding planetary movement
ca. 700	Isaiah dies

According to Isaiah 1:1, Isaiah served as a prophet during the reign of several kings in Judah, including Uzziah, Jotham, Ahaz, and Hezekiah. He had personal dealings with at least two of those kings. Many scholars believe that Isaiah's ministry took place between 740 and 700 (or perhaps 699) B.C.—approximately forty years.

Isaiah's name means "Jehovah is salvation." How fitting that a man who devoted his life to testifying of the saving power of the Messiah should have a name that witnesses his testimony.

Isaiah's wife is called "prophetess" in Isaiah's record, suggesting that she too had the gift of revelation (Isaiah 8:3). Isaiah and his wife had at least two sons who also served as signs to Israel. "Behold, I and the children whom the Lord hath given me are for signs and for wonders in Israel from the Lord of hosts" (v. 18).

The Kingdom of Judah at the Time of Isaiah

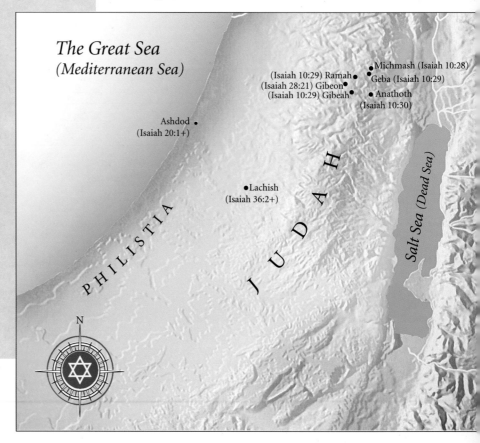

The Great Sea
(Mediterranean Sea)

Michmash (Isaiah 10:28)
(Isaiah 10:29) Ramah
Geba (Isaiah 10:29)
(Isaiah 28:21) Gibeon
(Isaiah 10:29) Gibeah
Anathoth (Isaiah 10:30)

Ashdod (Isaiah 20:1+)

Lachish (Isaiah 36:2+)

PHILISTIA

JUDAH

Salt Sea (Dead Sea)

N

Isaiah, by Gustave Doré (1832–1883). Woodcut (digitally colorized).
This illustration first appeared in the immensely popular French Bible *La Sainte Bible,* published in 1865. Doré took his work seriously by studying the Bible until he was satisfied that his artwork represented the scripture text itself.

Isaiah and His Children: "Signs and Wonders in Israel"

Footnote *a* of Isaiah 8:18 provides a translation of the names of Isaiah and his family members.

Name	Meaning	Significance
Isaiah (Isaiah 1:1)	"Jehovah is salvation"	Isaiah is a type of Jesus Christ, who brings salvation to those who accept him.
Shear-jashub, Isaiah's son (Isaiah 7:3)	"a remnant shall return"	This name represents a remnant of the people of Israel, which will return to their covenant lands. One remnant will return from Babylon; one will return in the last days.
Maher-shalal-hash-baz, Isaiah's son (Isaiah 8:3)	"speed, spoil, hasten, plunder"	This name represents (1) Assyria who would (with *speed* and *haste*) *spoil* and *plunder* ancient nations, (2) Jesus Christ who will (with *speed* and *haste*) *spoil* and *plunder* the nations at his second coming.

Above: An ancient feeding trough carved from stone, Megiddo. Often made from stone or wood, feeding troughs served domesticated beasts, including oxen, asses, and horses. Troughs are still used today but generally are made of metal.

The ox knoweth his owner, and the ass his master's [feeding trough]; but Israel doth not know, my people doth not consider.

The ox and ass are beasts of burden that need an owner's care and support. The Israelites, like the ox and ass, must rely on their master, God, for spiritual sustenance. The ox and ass are dumb animals, yet they still obey their master. The children of Israel do not always obey their master.

The terms "owner" and "master" are symbols that refer to the Lord, who is the owner and master of the people of Israel. The Hebrew for "owner" here means someone who has purchased an item rather than received it through other means such as inheriting it, being given it, or simply finding it. Christ is the purchaser. He purchased the church of God through his atoning sacrifice, accepting the role of caretaker and saving all humanity from sin and death. This idea is taught by Paul concerning the "church of God, which he [Jesus] hath purchased with his own blood" (Acts 20:28; 1 Corinthians 6:20).

Above: Oxen, like this one, standing near a feeding trough in Bethany, recognize their owner as well as their owner's feeding trough. Domestic oxen provided humans with milk, meat, and leather. They also served as beasts of burden.

Above: Two asses and a man, near Kibbutz Eilon. In biblical times, the ass was a common yet significant beast of burden that hauled goods and people.

ISAIAH 1:8

And the daughter of Zion is left as a cottage in a vineyard, as a lodge in a garden of cucumbers, as a besieged city.

The expression "daughter of Zion" refers to the city of Jerusalem as well as to its inhabitants (Lamentations 1:6–8; 2:10; Zechariah 9:9). All that remains in Jerusalem after its destruction are cottages and huts. Jerusalem, which once housed the mighty spiritual fortress—God's temple—is now like a cottage. This is a symbolic as well as a literal warning to those who forsake the Lord in the latter days.

Above and left: Huts at Neot Kedumim, a biblical landscape reserve. Temporary shelters were built in gardens or vineyards before harvest to house people who protected crops from fowl, beast, or man. Shelters were hastily made with inferior materials such as reeds, palm branches, or matting supported by wood poles. These huts began to sag and fall soon after the harvest.

Poetic Parallelisms

Isaiah consistently wrote in a form called poetic parallelism. In poetic parallelism, the writer makes a statement in a line, a phrase, or a sentence and then restates it, so that the second line, phrase, or sentence echoes the first.

There are approximately eleven hundred of these short poetic units in the book of Isaiah. Parallelisms help readers understand what Isaiah is trying to emphasize. They also serve to clarify his message. The first line of a parallelism presents a thought, then the second line restates it, often clarifying the words of the first. Note the following four parallelisms in Isaiah 1:2–3, with parallel words underlined or in bold. For example, in the first parallelism listed below, **hear** parallels **give ear** and **heavens** parallels **earth**.

Examples:

Hear, O <u>heavens,</u>
and **give ear,** O <u>earth:</u>

I have nourished and brought up <u>children,</u>
and <u>they</u> have rebelled against **me.**

The **ox** knoweth his <u>owner,</u>
and the **ass** his <u>master's</u> [feeding trough]:

but **Israel** doth not <u>know,</u>
my people doth not <u>consider.</u>

For, behold, the Lord, the Lord of hosts, doth take away from Jerusalem and from Judah the stay and the staff, the whole stay of bread, and the whole stay of water, . . . For Jerusalem is ruined, and Judah is fallen: because their tongue and their doings are against the Lord, to provoke the eyes of his glory.

Isaiah prophesies in this chapter that anarchy and ruin will come upon the inhabitants of Jerusalem and Judah because of their sinful nature (Isaiah 3:1–12).

He likens their sins to those committed in Sodom before its destruction: "The show of their countenance doth witness against them; and they declare their sin as Sodom, they hide it not." Isaiah adds, "Woe unto their soul! for they have rewarded evil unto themselves" (Isaiah 3:9).

Isaiah's words were certainly fulfilled, as history attests. Jerusalem was destroyed by the Babylonians in about 587 B.C. and again in A.D. 70 by the Romans. Despite Jerusalem's centuries of ruin, its citizens of the last days have much to look forward to. Isaiah prophesies that in the last days, Jerusalem's waste places will be rebuilt, and the Lord will comfort his people and redeem Jerusalem. Isaiah writes: "Break forth into joy, sing together, ye waste places of Jerusalem: for the Lord hath comforted his people, he hath redeemed Jerusalem" (Isaiah 52:9).

Above: A stand of grain. Barley and wheat were the two most common and important grains grown and harvested in ancient Israel. Both grains represented staple foods.

Left: Cistern at Jabal Sabir, North Yemen.

Above: Empty water cistern, Gibeon. Cisterns served as the main water source for many ancient villages and towns. Villagers built channels that collected winter rains into one or more cisterns. Water users would draw from the cistern for domestic purposes.

Above: The governments of Israel and Judah kept reserve supplies of grain, wine, oil, and weapons in store cities, such as Jerusalem, Beth Shemesh, and Megiddo. The empty grain storage of Megiddo is an example of one reserve.

Foods Mentioned by Isaiah

bread	3:1, 7
broth	65:4
butter	7:15, 22
corn	17:5; 21:10
drink	5:11
eggs	10:14; 59:5
feast(s)	5:12; 25:6
fig	34:4
grapes	17:6; 18:5
honey	7:15, 22
meal	47:2
meat	57:6
milk	7:22
oil	41:19
provender	30:24
roast	44:16
spices	39:2
water	3:1
wine(s)	1:22; 5:11

My wellbeloved hath a vineyard in a very fruit-ful hill: And he fenced it, and gathered out the stones thereof, and planted it with the choicest vine, and built a tower in the midst of it, and also made a winepress therein: and he looked that it should bring forth grapes, and it brought forth wild grapes.

These verses are part of the Song of the Vineyard. The song is about a caring master who shows great concern and love for his vineyard. The master is the Lord and the vineyard is the house of Israel, the Lord's covenant people. Grapes become plump, juicy, and sweet when the master of the vineyard has planted them in a fertile hill, removed stones and weeds, and prepared for the harvest. Members of the house of Israel, too, can flourish with the master's care.

Those who do not respond to care, however, become like wild or rotten grapes, which symbolize corrupt or evil people (Hosea 9:10). They will not partake of the atonement and abide in Christ. They will be trodden down by the Lord in great fury at his second coming, staining his robe red (D&C 133:50–51).

Those who follow Christ will bring forth good fruit (John 15). God made Israel the "choicest vine" so that it would be fruitful and become a righteous people among the nations. He built a tower in the vineyard so that watchmen, including the prophets, could watch for impending danger and then warn the children of Israel (Ezekiel 3:17; 33:1–7; D&C 101:43–62). He also made a winepress in anticipation of a great harvest.

Jesus Speaks of Isaiah

3 Nephi 23:1

"Yea, a commandment I give unto you that ye search [the words of Isaiah] diligently."

3 Nephi 23:1

"Great are the words of Isaiah."

3 Nephi 23:2

"[Isaiah] spake as touching all things concerning my people which are of the house of Israel."

3 Nephi 23:3

"All things that [Isaiah] spake have been and shall be."

Top left: A large vineyard located between Jerusalem and Hebron. The Holy Land was celebrated for its wine cultivation, as evidenced by frequent reference to vineyards, grapes, and wine throughout the Old Testament. Isaiah 5:1–2 summarizes the work of preparing a vineyard, which involved making a winepress, frequently hewn from solid rock. Harvested grapes were eaten as fresh fruit, dried into raisins, or prepared and fermented for wine.

Middle left: An ancient winepress. After grapes were harvested, they were carried in baskets to a grape press. There, individuals trod on the grapes so that the juice flowed into a vat, where it was gathered into containers.

Left: The Gihon Spring at the entrance of Hezekiah's Tunnel, Jerusalem. The Gihon Spring flows from a natural cave on the west side of the valley of Kidron, south of where Solomon's temple once stood. In the Old Testament period, the spring was the chief source of water for Jerusalem's inhabitants.

Solomon was anointed king near this spring in a sacred ceremony. Perhaps other kings were anointed here as well. From this spring King Hezekiah's engineers ran a tunnel under the city to safeguard Jerusalem's water supply from the invading Assyrians. The Gihon Spring is likely the "upper pool" mentioned by Isaiah.

ISAIAH 7:3

Then said the Lord unto Isaiah, Go forth now to meet Ahaz, thou, and Shear-jashub thy son, at the end of the conduit of the upper pool in the highway of the fuller's field.

Shear-jashub was a son of Isaiah and the prophetess and the elder brother of Maher-shalal-hash-baz. In Hebrew, his name means "a remnant shall return." (For examples of other names that are signs, see Hosea 1:6–9.) As his name suggests, the boy was to become a living symbol to the Jews (Isaiah 8:18), a reminder to the Israelites that a remnant would return to their land and their God (Isaiah 6:11–13).

The Lord commanded Isaiah to take Shear-jashub with him to meet King Ahaz at the upper pool, probably near the Gihon Spring in the valley of Kidron. Ahaz may have been at the pool with his officers to check Jerusalem's water supply in anticipation of the siege by Assyria. The Lord, who knew Ahaz's location, inspired Isaiah and his son to go there.

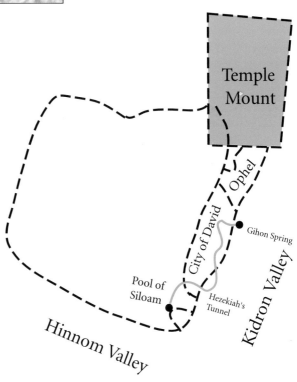

Jerusalem's Water System at the Time of Isaiah
Gihon Spring, Hezekiah's Tunnel, and Siloam Pool.

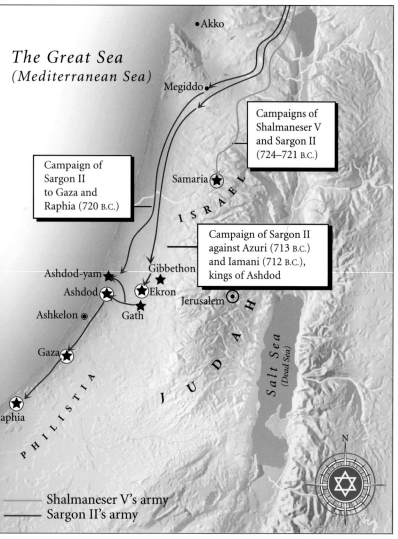

The Great Sea
(Mediterranean Sea)

•Akko

Megiddo•

Campaigns of
Shalmaneser V
and Sargon II
(724–721 B.C.)

Campaign of
Sargon II
to Gaza and
Raphia (720 B.C.)

Samaria ★

ISRAEL

Campaign of Sargon II
against Azuri (713 B.C.)
and Iamani (712 B.C.),
kings of Ashdod

Ashdod-yam ★
Gibbethon ★
Ashdod ★
★ Ekron
Jerusalem ◉
Ashkelon ◉
Gath ★

JUDAH

Salt Sea
(Dead Sea)

Gaza ★

PHILISTIA

Raphia ★

N

—— Shalmaneser V's army
—— Sargon II's army

Campaigns of Shalmaneser V and Sargon II (Isaiah 20)
Adapted from *Macmillan Bible Atlas,* 149

*Within threescore and five years shall Ephraim
be broken, that it be not a people.*

What was happening in the political world of
Isaiah's time? Assyria, the enemy of Israel, had
embarked on a ruthless campaign to expand its bor-
ders. Isaiah's specific prophecy that in "threescore and
five years" Ephraim, or the northern kingdom of
Israel, would no longer be a kingdom or a nation was
fulfilled. Ephraim fell in 721 B.C., midway through
Isaiah's ministry.

King Sargon II of Assyria deported most of
Ephraim's citizens, some of the ten tribes of Israel, to
the north countries. The author of the book of Kings
reports on the attack on Samaria, the capital of the
northern kingdoms: "Then the king of Assyria came
up throughout all the land, and went up to Samaria,
and besieged it three years. In the ninth year of
Hoshea the king of Assyria took Samaria, and carried
Israel away into Assyria" (2 Kings 17:5–6).

The deportation of ancient Israel occurred because of the people's great sins. "For so it was, that the
children of Israel had sinned against the Lord their God
. . . And walked in the statutes of the heathen. . . . And
the children of Israel did secretly those things that
were not right against the Lord their God" (vv. 7–10).
Years later King Sennacherib campaigned against
Judah, defeating many cities and villages, and again
deporting many of its citizens.

Left: This relief carving is one of a series on the walls of an ancient palace
in Nineveh, Assyria's capital. The carving depicts prisoners of war after
Sennacherib's siege of Lachish, a fortified city in the kingdom of Judah. The
siege took place during the latter part
of Isaiah's lifetime, 701 B.C. The relief
depicts two women and four children—
two young girls and two seated infants.
They are Israelites who were deported
from their homeland. The dress of the
prisoners of war probably reflects
Israelite clothing of the period.

ISAIAH 9:9–10

And all the people shall know, even Ephraim and the inhabitant of Samaria, that say in the pride and stoutness of heart, The bricks are fallen down, but we will build with hewn stones: the sycomores are cut down, but we will change them into cedars.

In Isaiah chapters 9 and 10, the prophet foretells the doom of the northern kingdom of Israel because of its great pride. The Lord's word, which applies to both ancient and modern Israel, has been given to the house of Israel through the prophets (Isaiah 9:8). Because the people do not seek the Lord, and because they are hypocrites, lie, and do evil, he will destroy all levels of society, including its leaders, followers, false prophets, and young men (vv. 13–17).

Verses 18 and 19 describe this destruction by fire with such terms as "burneth," "fire," "devour," "kindle," "mount up like the lifting up of," "land darkened" (perhaps because of the smoke), and "fuel of the fire." In addition, social chaos will rule and brotherly love will not be found, for family will fight against family, and tribe will war against tribe (vv. 19–21). Those who make unrighteous and oppressive laws as well as those who forget the poor, the widows, and the fatherless will also suffer at the day of judgment and will be among the captives or slain. They will not be able to flee for help to other sources such as idols or other nations. (Isaiah 10:1–4)

In Isaiah 9:9–10, the Lord speaks specifically regarding the pride of the people. They speak with "pride and stoutness of heart." The people believe that if they are destroyed, then they will rebuild their homes with stronger, hewn stones and they will replant with finer trees, such as cedars.

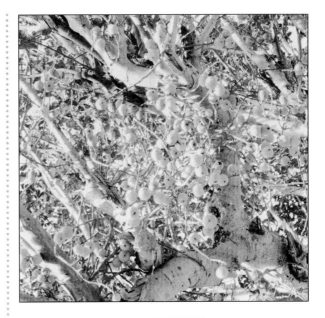

Above: The fruit of a sycomore tree is abundant and nearly ripe, Jericho. The sycomore is a fruit-bearing tree valued for its figs and lumber. The Egyptians used its wood to make coffins, but apparently sycomore wood was not as precious as that of a cedar (Isaiah 9:10). The sycomore grows to a height of forty feet. Its branches spread widely from a short trunk.

Right: Fallen bricks with hewn stones in the background at Hisham's Palace, near Jericho. In Isaiah's time, bricks were made of mud or clay mixed with sand, straw, or other material, and then baked in a kiln or dried by the sun. Bricks were inferior to hewn stone because bricks were more breakable. Additionally, hewn stone was more expensive to prepare.

Jerusalem's inhabitants prepared for impending war against the armies of Elam and Kir by building up a weapons inventory, fortifying the city's walls, taking a census to determine how many men of fighting age were available to defend the city, and preparing the city's water supply (Isaiah 22:8–11). The "lower pool" mentioned in verse 9 refers to the pool at the southern end of Hezekiah's Tunnel, an engineering marvel that permitted Jerusalem's inhabitants to safely obtain water during a siege.

Jerusalem relied for security on its weapons and preparations for war rather than on its Maker. In a pivotal clause Isaiah states: "But ye have not looked unto the maker thereof" (v. 11). Jehovah is the Maker (Hosea 8:14; D&C 30:2), the great Architect who fashioned Jerusalem long ago. Isaiah's words compare God, who was the city's original builder, to those who attempted to build Jerusalem through repairs, fortifications, and water channels.

During this period of impending battle, Judah should have been fasting, praying, worshiping in the temple, and seeking God's word through the prophets. Note the terminology Isaiah uses as he explains Judah's reliance on worldly might instead of heavenly powers. Jerusalem's inhabitants did "look" to their armories (Isaiah 22:8), but they had "not looked unto" Jehovah, their Maker (v. 11).

Announcement of Judgment

Isaiah prophesies judgment, doom, or destruction against the following peoples or nations because of their pride and wickedness. An announcement sometimes lists sins as well as the manner in which people will be doomed or destroyed.

Jerusalem and Judah	3:1–12; 29:1–10; 51:17–20
The daughters of Zion	3:16–4:1
The wicked	5:8–25; 30:27–33; 33:7–14
The northern kingdom of Israel	9:8–10:4
Assyria	10:12–19
Babylon	13:6–22; 21:1–10; 47
The Philistines	14:29–32
Moab	15:1–16:4
Damascus and Israel	17:1–11
The nations that oppress Israel	17:12–14
Egypt	19:1–22
Dumah	21:11–12
Arabia	21:13–17
The valley of vision (Jerusalem)	22:1–14
Tyre	23:1–14
Ephraim	28:1–8
The beasts of the south	30:6–7
Edom	34:1–15
The world	63:1–6

Above left: Hezekiah's Tunnel. King Hezekiah anticipated a drawn-out Assyrian siege against Jerusalem. He secured Jerusalem's water supplies by boring a long tunnel beneath the city, allowing for a source of water within the city walls. The tunnel represents a significant engineering feat, as it was excavated out of solid rock with picks and other rudimentary tools.

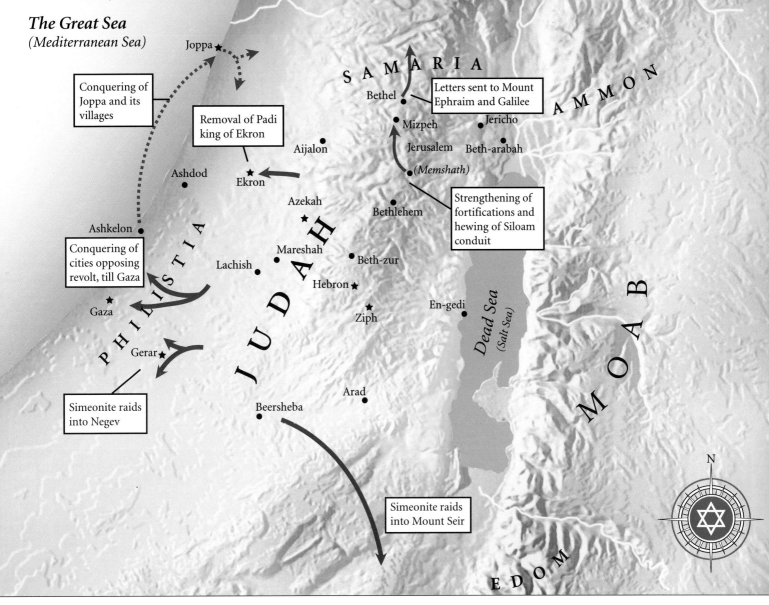

Preparations of Hezekiah for Rebellion against Assyria, 705 to 701 B.C. (Isaiah 22:8–11)
Adapted from *Macmillan Bible Atlas,* 152

Inscription inside Hezekiah's Tunnel

The builders of Hezekiah's Tunnel in Jerusalem recorded their success in an inscription on the wall of the tunnel. The tunnel and inscription were completed ca. 701 B.C., shortly before Isaiah's death. The inscription, in part, reads: "When the tunnel was driven through, the quarrymen hewed [the rock], each man toward his fellow, axe against axe; and the water flowed from the spring toward the reservoir for 1,200 cubits, and the height of the rock above the head[s] of the quarrymen was one hundred cubits."

Source: James B. Pritchard, *Ancient Near Eastern Texts: Relating to the Old Testament,* 321.

Sargon II Conquers Some of the Ten Tribes

Assyrian kings often had accounts of their war deeds and triumphs recorded on clay tablets, stone slabs, or palace walls. These royal inscriptions were designed to inform future generations of the greatness and might of the kings. In this Assyrian royal inscription, Sargon II (721–705 B.C.), king of Assyria, records his invasion of Samaria and the northern kingdom of Israel.

"I [Sargon] besieged and conquered Samaria, . . . led away as booty 27,290 inhabitants of it. . . . I conquered and sacked the towns Shinuhtu (and) Samaria, and all Israel."

Source: James B. Pritchard, *Ancient Near Eastern Texts: Relating to the Old Testament,* 284–85.

By this therefore shall the iniquity of Jacob be purged . . . when he maketh all the stones of the altar as chalkstones that are beaten in sunder, the groves and images shall not stand up.

Isaiah gives the sign by which it will be known that the people of Jacob, or the house of Israel, will be purged of sin. Jacob will crush the stones of the altars of false worship into pieces as if they were chalk stone and knock down the groves and images.

Chalk stone is a soft stone that crumbles easily and quickly dissolves in rain. Beaten chalk stone symbolizes the complete destruction of the altars of idolatry. When Israel's inhabitants destroy all forms of idolatry and false worship from their land and hearts, as if making all the stones of the idolatrous altars into chalk stone, then their iniquity will also be purged.

Above: A pile of beaten chalk stone in a cave near Bet Guvrin National Park. Crushed, heated chalk or limestone was employed anciently to make plaster. The plaster was used for lining the inner and outer walls of homes and public buildings and for waterproofing cisterns and water channels.

Above left: Chalk in its natural form. Bet Guvrin National Park.

The Northern Kingdom of Israel at the Time of Isaiah

The Great Sea
(Mediterranean Sea)

• Tyre
(Isaiah 23:1+)

BASHAN
(Isaiah 33:9)

Mt. Carmel
(Isaiah 33:9+)

Plain of Sharon (Isaiah 33:9)

Jordan River

• Samaria
(Isaiah 10:9+)

ISRAEL
(Isaiah 1:3+)

AMMON
(Isaiah 11:14)

Ramah • • Geba
(Isaiah 10:29) (Isaiah 10:29)

• Jerusalem

• Ashdod
(Isaiah 20:1) JUDAH

Salt Sea
(Dead Sea)

N

ISAIAH 28:1

Woe to the crown of pride, to the drunkards of Ephraim, whose glorious beauty is a fading flower.

Isaiah denounces the northern kingdom, Ephraim, pronouncing upon its people woe, or severe anguish and distress, resulting from God's judgments. The "crown of pride" is Samaria, the capital of Ephraim. Its walled city stood on a hill, perhaps presenting the image of a crown, and its people were full of pride (Isaiah 9:9).

Isaiah accuses Samaria of drunkenness (Isaiah 28:1, 3), and Ephraim is also singled out for drunkenness in Hosea 7:5, 14. Not simply literal drunkenness is condemned here but also the spiritual drunkenness of sin and apostasy. Samaria was a flourishing and glorious community, but its time of glory passed away like a fading flower.

Above: A fading flower near the Garden Tomb, Jerusalem.

Prophetic Speech Forms

Prophetic speech forms are important literary devices found in Isaiah's writings. They are an example of "the manner of prophesying among the Jews" (2 Nephi 25:1). These forms are also found in the writings of Hosea, Ezekiel, Moses, Nephi, Alma, Joseph Smith, and others. Prophetic speech forms are brief revelatory statements that follow a set formula. They frequently contain the name of God, are located at the beginning or the end of a revelation, and indicate prophetic authority. Those who are not prophets may not appropriately use these forms, for the authority attached to them originates from God.

Of course, revelations may lack such a formula and still have power and authority from God. But the speech forms aid our understanding of the scriptures and suggest that Isaiah wrote according to an ancient pattern given by the Lord.

The Messenger Formula

"Thus saith the Lord." This formula is found forty-six times in the writings of Isaiah. Its purpose is to set forth both the divine authority and the origin of the revelation.

The Revelation Formula

"The word that Isaiah, son of Amoz, saw" or "The Lord spake also unto me again, saying." This form likewise indicates prophetic authority and the source of the revelation.

The Proclamation Formula

"Hearken unto me" or "Hear the word of the Lord." This form's primary function is to call people to attention so that they can hear what the Lord wants to say to them through his prophet.

The Oath Formula

"As the Lord liveth" or "The Lord of hosts hath sworn." With this declaration the Lord essentially says, "As surely as I live, so surely will these prophecies come to pass," or "This will happen because I say it will, and I never lie."

The Woe Oracle

"Oracle" means words of revelation from God. This form can easily be recognized by the use of the word "woe" one or more times within the oracle, e.g., "Woe unto the wicked!" or "Woe to the crown of pride."

Source: Adapted from Donald W. Parry, Jay A. Parry, and Tina M. Peterson, *Understanding Isaiah,* 599–600.

Moab at the Time of Isaiah

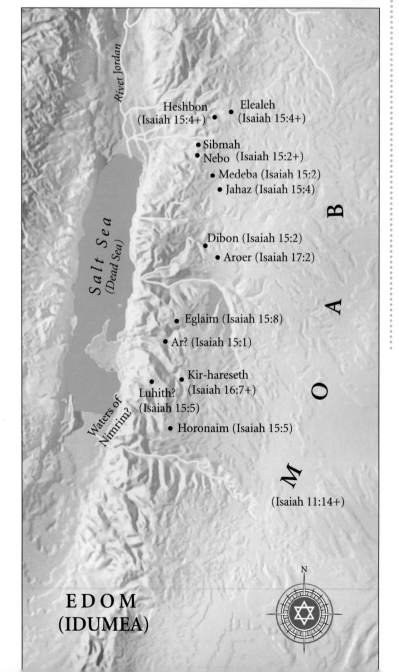

Moab at the Time of Isaiah

River Jordan

Heshbon
(Isaiah 15:4+)

Elealeh
(Isaiah 15:4+)

Sibmah

Nebo (Isaiah 15:2+)

Medeba (Isaiah 15:2)

Jahaz (Isaiah 15:4)

Salt Sea
(Dead Sea)

Dibon (Isaiah 15:2)

Aroer (Isaiah 17:2)

B

Eglaim (Isaiah 15:8)

Ar? (Isaiah 15:1)

A

Kir-hareseth
(Isaiah 16:7+)

Luhith?
(Isaiah 15:5)

O

Waters of Nimrim?

Horonaim (Isaiah 15:5)

M

(Isaiah 11:14+)

EDOM
(IDUMEA)

N

ISAIAH 30:13

Therefore this iniquity shall be to you as a breach ready to fall, swelling out in a high wall, whose breaking cometh suddenly at an instant.

Isaiah compares ancient Judah's iniquity to a large crack in the outside wall that protects Jerusalem. The crack expands, weakening the wall until it suddenly crumbles. Similarly, Judah's inhabitants have been weakened through sin. Their iniquity increases, like the crack in the wall, until their enemies are able to enter through the breach and destroy their nation. This excellent description illustrates the effect of sin on all. Even a little sin, not repented of, can be like a crack in a wall, which can grow larger and larger until it leads to spiritual destruction.

ISAIAH 30:14

And he shall break it as the breaking of the potters' vessel that is broken in pieces; he shall not spare: so that there shall not be found in the bursting of it a sherd to take fire from the hearth, or to take water withal out of the pit.

In Isaiah 30:1–17, the prophet lists sins of ancient Judah. The nation does not take counsel from the Lord, does not pray to the Lord, trusts Egypt and its horses rather than the Lord, carries its riches to Egypt, rejects the prophets and seers and desires them to prophesy "smooth things" and lies, and despises God's word.

In verse 14, Isaiah likens the destruction of Judah to a shattered clay vessel that can no longer serve its original purpose. Not a single shard, a fragment of the shattered vessel, is large enough to serve as a scoop "to take fire from the hearth" or "to take water" from a pool. Similarly, Judah's sinful inhabitants are not suitable to serve as God's holy people in any way.

Above left: Breach in a wall, east of Hebron. Stone walls, common in antiquity, are still used in modern times throughout the Near East. Sometimes, usually years after the wall's construction, its stones bulge out or fall, causing a breach, as shown in the picture. The breach is caused by plants forcing their way through the stones, by erosion, or by other natural forces.

"I will bless those who bless you... And in you all the families of the earth shall be blessed."

Genesis 12:3

pray
for the peace of Jerusalem.

May they prosper who love you. May peace be within your walls. Psalm 122:6,7

Lift up the Jewish people facing scorn, ridicule and persecution around the world.

Intercede for Jews who are fleeing persecution right now in the former Soviet Union and much of the Muslim world.

Pray for the peace of Jerusalem. Ask God to protect the Jewish people in their homeland. Pray against terrorism. Pray for strength and courage for the people of Israel.

Ask God to equip Chosen People Ministries as our workers minister God's love and peace to Jews immigrating to Germany, Israel and the United States.

Pray that God will open a door for the Gospel to the hearts of Jews as Chosen People missionaries reach out in ten countries.

Ask God to use our ministry resources — including the Internet — to touch the hearts of Jews with the Gospel.

Thank you and God bless you for your prayers!

Chosen People Ministries
www.chosen-people.com

ISAIAH 32:14

Because the palaces shall be forsaken; the multitude of the city shall be left; the forts and towers shall be for dens for ever, a joy of wild asses, a pasture of flocks.

Isaiah prophesies of a time when palaces and cities are forsaken and left desolate, and forts and towers become dwelling places for animals. He is probably referring to the city of Jerusalem and the kingdom of Judah during the Babylonian captivity and exile. During this period, Jerusalem's inhabitants were killed, forced to flee, or taken captive, and the once crowded city was partially abandoned. The fortifications and towers throughout Judah became dwelling places for animals.

Above: A cow finding pasture at the ruins of an ancient tower near Caesarea Philippi.

Left: Broken pottery near Beth-Shemesh. As archaeologists excavate ancient biblical sites, they uncover hundreds of pieces of broken pottery from the remains of both public and private buildings. These pieces of pottery are gathered into a single location and then studied and cataloged for research purposes. The more interesting or rare pieces are shipped to laboratories or museums. The more common pieces are discarded, as shown here.

Occupations and Trades

artificer	3:3	harvestman	17:5	smith	44:12; 54:16
astrologers	47:13	hireling	16:14; 21:16	sower	55:10
carpenter	41:7; 44:13	lender	24:2	teachers	30:20; 43:27
creditors	50:1	merchant(s)	23:2, 8	traffickers	23:8
exactors	60:17	plowman/men	28:24; 61:5	treaders (wine)	16:10
feller	14:8	potter	29:16; 30:14	vinedressers	61:5
fishers	19:8	prognosticators	47:13	workman/men	40:19–20
fishing	19:5–8	shearers	53:7		
goldsmith	40:19; 41:7	shepherd(s)	13:20; 31:4		

Above: The high place at Tel Dan, now in ruins, was a well-known religious site during the biblical period. High places were man-made platforms or shrines used for various religious rites, which often included animal sacrifice. The high places and altars that King Hezekiah destroyed belonged to religious systems that worshiped idols and false gods.

King Hezekiah—Like a Bird in a Cage

In an Assyrian royal inscription, Sennacherib, king of Assyria, boasts of taking Hezekiah prisoner.

"As to Hezekiah, the Jew, he did not submit to my yoke, I laid seige to 46 of his strong cities, walled forts and to the countless small villages in their vicinity, and conquered (them) by means of well-stamped (earth–) ramps, and battering-rams brought (thus) near (to the walls) (combined with) the attack by foot soldiers, (using) mines, breeches as well as sapper work. I drove out (of them) 200,150 people, young and old, male and female, horses, mules, donkeys, camels, big and small cattle beyond counting, and considered (them) booty. Himself I made a prisoner in Jerusalem, his royal residence, like a bird in a cage."

Source: James B. Pritchard, *Ancient Near Eastern Texts: Relating to the Old Testament,* 288.

ISAIAH 36:7

Is it not he, whose high places and whose altars Hezekiah hath taken away?

The son of Ahaz and Abi, Hezekiah became king at twenty-five and reigned twenty-nine years. Hezekiah was a righteous man who "did that which was right in the sight of the Lord . . . and departed not from following him, but kept his commandments" (2 Kings 18:3, 6). As king, Hezekiah made a number of religious reforms among his people. He "removed the high places, and brake the images, and cut down the groves, and brake in pieces the brasen serpent that Moses had made: for unto those days the children of Israel did burn incense to it" (2 Kings 18:4). Because of his righteousness and religious reforms, the author of 2 Kings wrote this tribute to him: "He trusted in the Lord God of Israel; so that after him was none like him among all the kings of Judah, nor any that were before him" (2 Kings 18:5).

And Hezekiah went up unto the house of the Lord. And Hezekiah prayed unto the Lord.

While tens of thousands of Assyrian soldiers waited to destroy Jerusalem's inhabitants, Hezekiah petitioned the Lord through prayer. In the house of the Lord, he prayed, "O Lord of hosts, God of Israel, that dwellest between the cherubims, thou art the God, even thou alone, of all the kingdoms of the earth: thou hast made heaven and earth. Incline thine ear, O Lord, and hear; open thine eyes, O Lord, and see: and hear all the words of Sennacherib, which hath sent to reproach the living God. Of a truth, Lord, the kings of Assyria have laid waste all the nations, and their countries" (Isaiah 37:16–18).

In response to Hezekiah's humble prayer, the Lord sent his prophet Isaiah to the king and promised deliverance from the Assyrians. Isaiah assured Hezekiah that Jerusalem's inhabitants need not fear, for the Lord would not permit the Assyrians to enter the city of Jerusalem (v. 34). The Lord heard Hezekiah's prayer and sent an angel, who destroyed 185,000 men in the Assyrian camp, saving Hezekiah and his people (v. 36).

Members of the Church of Jesus Christ of Latter-day Saints today may liken this passage from Isaiah to themselves. All Saints may go to the temple with their cares and challenges, whether small or great, and seek God's help through prayer. He will provide answers to their prayers and bless their lives, just as he did for Hezekiah and the inhabitants of Jerusalem.

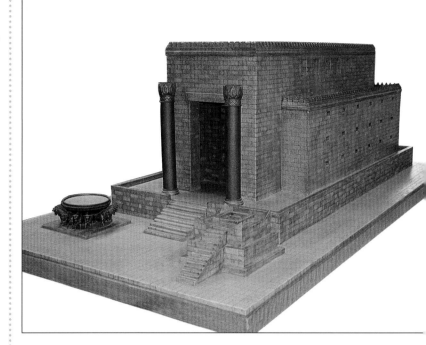

Above and right: Model of Solomon's temple, showing laver, sacrificial altar, and two pillars at the entrance. The Temple of Solomon was an imposing structure on Mount Moriah, Jerusalem. Hewn stone, gold, silver, bronze, cedars of Lebanon, and other precious materials were used to decorate and beautify the house of the Lord. Isaiah worshiped in this temple, and King Hezekiah sought the Lord's counsel here during the Assyrian siege.

Assyrian Royal Inscriptions Referring to Kings of Israel and Judah

Date	Kings of Israel	Kings of Assyria	Context
738 B.C.	Menahem	Tiglath-pileser III	Menahem pays tribute to Tiglath-pileser III
732 B.C.	Pekah	Tiglath-pileser III	Tiglath-pileser III overthrows Pekah
732 B.C.	Hoshea	Tiglath-pileser III	Tiglath-pileser III puts Hoshea on throne

Date	Kings of Judah	Kings of Assyria	Context
732 B.C.	Ahaz	Tiglath-pileser III	Ahaz pays tribute to Tiglath-pileser III
701 B.C.	Hezekiah	Sennacherib	Hezekiah pays tribute to Sennacherib
?	Manasseh	Esarhaddon	Manasseh pays tribute to Esarhaddon

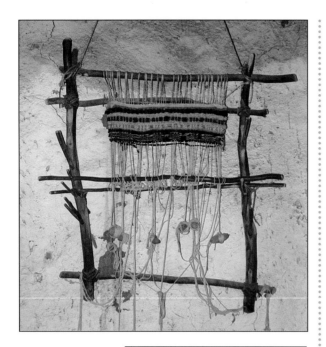

Above: This weaving loom at Qatzrin, an ancient village from the talmudic period (ca. A.D. 200–500), may resemble ancient looms.

Hezekiah's Psalm

After King Hezekiah, sick and near death, learned that the Lord had postponed his death, he wrote the following psalm. The psalm portrays Hezekiah's humility, meekness, and reliance upon the Lord.

Isaiah 38:17–20

Behold, for peace I had great bitterness:
but thou hast in love to my soul delivered it from the pit of corruption,
for thou hast cast all my sins behind thy back.
For the grave cannot praise thee,
death cannot celebrate thee:
they that go down into the pit cannot hope for thy truth.
The living, the living, he shall praise thee, as I do this day:
the father to the children shall make known thy truth.
The Lord was ready to save me:
therefore we will sing my songs to the stringed instruments
all the days of our life in the house of the Lord.

Right: Dovecote from the biblical era, Bet Guvrin National Park. Dovecotes are structures with several compartments used to house domestic pigeons. In the biblical world, dovecotes were often carved out of the limestone walls of underground caves.

Far right: Egyptian children weaving a rug, Cairo. The art of weaving also existed in Isaiah's time.

ISAIAH 38:12–14

Mine age is departed, and is removed from me as a shepherd's tent: I have cut off like a weaver my life: he will cut me off with pining sickness: from day even to night wilt thou make an end of me. . . . Like a crane or a swallow, so did I chatter: I did mourn as a dove: mine eyes fail with looking upward.

Isaiah 38:1–8 relates that Hezekiah, king of Judah, is sick to the point that he will soon die. The Lord has warned him, "Set thine house in order: for thou shalt die, and not live" (v. 1). After Hezekiah prayed and wept much, the Lord showed mercy unto him and postponed his death for fifteen years. The king, to show his gratitude to the Lord, wrote a psalm portraying his humility, meekness, and reliance upon the Lord (vv. 9–20). The two verses cited above are part of his psalm.

The king writes: "Mine age is departed, and is removed from me as a shepherd's tent: I have cut off like a weaver my life." Hezekiah means that his life would end as easily as a shepherd dismantles his tent or as quickly as a weaver cuts and gathers finished fabric from a loom. The expression "like a crane or a swallow, so did I chatter: I did mourn as a dove" indicates that Hezekiah's pleadings with the Lord were at times loud, as a crane's cry, at other times soft, as a swallow's chirp, and on occasion mournful, as a dove's cooing.

Above: This reproduction of Herod's temple is at the Holy Land Hotel, Jerusalem. Although larger and more elaborate, its appearance is similar to the temple that was rebuilt when Cyrus, king of Persia, permitted the exiled Jews to return to and rebuild Jerusalem. Zerubbabel, the governor of Judah, oversaw the temple project.

Josephus Praises Isaiah

The Jewish historian Josephus, born about A.D. 37, described Isaiah in his history of the Jews.

"Now as to this prophet [Isaiah], he was by the confession of all, a divine and wonderful man in speaking truth; and out of the assurance that he had never written what was false, he wrote down all his prophecies, and left them behind him in books, that their accomplishment might be judged of from the events by posterity."

Source: *Antiquities of the Jews,* 10.2.35.

ISAIAH 44:28

I am the Lord . . . that saith of Cyrus, He is my shepherd, and shall perform all my pleasure: even saying to Jerusalem, Thou shalt be built; and to the temple, Thy foundation shall be laid.

Isaiah prophesies concerning Cyrus approximately two hundred years before Cyrus ruled Babylon. Cyrus was the king who freed the people of Israel from political bondage and provided a way for them to return to their homeland to rebuild Jerusalem and the temple.

Interestingly, the Jewish historian Josephus, writing only a few years after the crucifixion of Christ, recorded how Cyrus learned that he should permit the Jews to return to Jerusalem to rebuild the temple. "This was known to Cyrus by his reading the book which Isaiah left behind him of his prophecies; for this prophet said that God had spoken thus to him in a secret vision: —'My will is, that Cyrus, whom I have appointed to be king over many and great nations, send back my people to their own land, and build my temple.' This was foretold by Isaiah one hundred and forty years before the temple was demolished. Accordingly, when Cyrus read this, and admired the divine power, an earnest desire and ambition seized upon him to fulfil what was so written" (*Antiquities of the Jews,* 11.1.1–2).

All that the Lord promised concerning Cyrus was accomplished, including the rebuilding of Jerusalem and its temple (2 Chronicles 36:23; Ezra 1:1–2; Isaiah 46:10).

ISAIAH 63:11–14

Where is he that put his holy Spirit within him? . . . That led them through the deep, as an horse in the wilderness, that they should not stumble? As a beast goeth down into the valley, the Spirit of the Lord caused him to rest: so didst thou lead thy people, to make thyself a glorious name.

Above: Addaxes graze at Hai-Bar Yotvata Nature Reserve, south of the Dead Sea. Such wildlife also existed at the time of Isaiah.

This passage is part of the Psalm of Mercy (Isaiah 63:7–14). This beautiful psalm shows the Lord's loving-kindness, great goodness, and mercy to the repentant. Isaiah notes that the Lord claims faithful Israel as his people and his children. He was not only a father but a Savior (v. 8). He bore their afflictions, redeemed them "in his love and in his pity," and carried them in their time of need (v. 9).

The faithful of Israel remember the Lord's goodness to their ancestors in the time of Moses. He had led them (an idea repeated three times in vv. 11–13) and blessed them with his Spirit and, by implication, he will do so again (v. 14).

Isaiah's image of a horse in the wilderness creates a beautiful comparison with the Lord's leading the children of Israel through the wilderness. The horse symbolizes how the Lord took ancient Israel safely through the deep, or the waters of the Red Sea. A horse in the wilderness is sure and steady of foot, especially when it is being led. In the same way, the Lord helped Israel to flee Egypt into the wilderness with steadiness, without faltering. The valley represents a place where beasts find water and grass, the sustenance they need. In the same way, the Lord makes all his children to "lie down in green pastures" (Psalm 23:2). While in the valley the Lord gave ancient Israel rest from bondage, rest from care, peace of heart, and peace of conscience, which are gifts of the Spirit. He will do the same for all his righteous children, in any age.

Above: A horse pastures at Hai-Bar Yotvata Nature Reserve. Horses were used in war during biblical times because of their speed, stamina, and intelligence. They were used principally to pull chariots, although they were sometimes ridden. Horses' sure-footedness in many types of terrain gave horsemen confidence.

ANCIENT ISRAEL'S NEIGHBORS

Isaiah was God's prophet who was called to preach, teach, and prophesy to the entire known world, not just to those who lived in his kingdom. He prophesied to Arabia (Isaiah 21:13–17), Assyria (10:12–19), Babylon (13:6–22; 21:1–10; 47:1–15), Edom (34:1–15), Egypt (19:1–25), Ethiopia (20:1–6), Moab (15:1–16:4), and Philistia (14:28–32).

Sunrise at Sinai.

And upon all the ships of Tarshish, and upon all pleasant pictures . . .

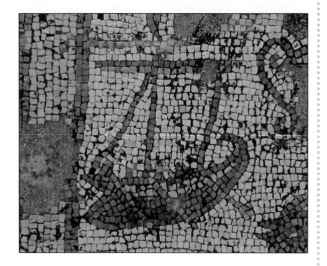

Above: This Byzantine mosaic of a ship, found in Hisham's Palace near Jericho, may be similar in appearance to the ships of Tarshish.

Tarshish, the precise location of which is unknown, was probably a prosperous and bustling Mediterranean seaport. Through Tarshish, Solomon imported luxury items, including gold, silver, ivory, apes, and peacocks (1 Kings 10:22). Perhaps because of the city's wealth and affluence, the destruction of Tarshish and its ships symbolizes the Lord's judgment on the proud and arrogant (Psalm 48:7; Isaiah 23:1, 14).

And it shall come to pass in that day, that the Lord shall hiss for the fly that is in the uttermost part of the rivers of Egypt, and for the bee that is in the land of Assyria.

Above: A tradition relates that bee-keepers of the ancient Near East called their bees by a whistle or hiss. The bees would then gather at their hives, usually made of clay or baskets. This tradition may have been known to those who heard Isaiah prophesy that the Lord would whistle for the fly and the bee.

Right: An ancient razor, without its handle, on display at an antiquities store, Jerusalem.

The fly and the bee often symbolize fighting soldiers (Deuteronomy 1:44; Psalm 118:12). These symbols are well chosen because "the flooding of the Nile brought . . . swarms of flies," and "the hill districts of Assyria were well known for their bees" (J. Alec Motyer, *The Prophecy of Isaiah: An Introduction and Commentary*, 89).

In this case, Isaiah prophesies that the Lord will prompt the Assyrian armies, here referred to as "bees," to come down on Judah. Judah's punishment comes because of wickedness. That the "Lord shall hiss" to the bees is a symbol built on an actual ancient practice. The word "hiss" can also mean whistle (Isaiah 5:30). Cyrillus of Alexandria (ca. A.D. 400) wrote about beekeepers who whistled to bees to get them to return to their hives (John D. Watts, *Isaiah 1–33*, 107).

In the same day shall the Lord shave with a razor that is hired . . . by them beyond the river, by the king of Assyria, the head, and the hair of the feet: and it shall also consume the beard.

Above: A model of a Canaanite merchant ship. During the Old Testament period, ships carried a variety of goods for merchants and seamen for navies. The Phoenicians, especially, were famous for their transport of merchandise on elaborately built ships to Mediterranean seaports.

Isaiah prophesies that Assyria will invade Israel (Isaiah 7:17–25). His prophecy, set forth in symbolic terms, declares that Assyria would occupy the entire land. Assyria's intent would be to humiliate and strip Israel of its dignity, make it poverty-stricken, and deport its citizens from the land. Isaiah records that the Lord would use a razor to shave the head, beard, and hair of the feet of members of the house of Israel. The razor represents the Assyrian king and his armies who customarily forced war prisoners to become slaves, and then humiliated and dishonored them by shaving them from head to toe.

The Assyrian invasion came upon members of the house of Israel because most of the people rejected the Lord and turned to idolatry and other gross sins.

**Egypt at the
Time of Isaiah**

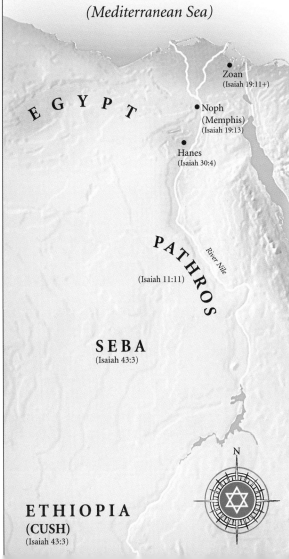

(Mediterranean Sea)

EGYPT

Zoan
(Isaiah 19:11+)

Noph
(Memphis)
(Isaiah 19:13)

Hanes
(Isaiah 30:4)

PATHROS

River Nile

(Isaiah 11:11)

SEBA
(Isaiah 43:3)

N

ETHIOPIA
(CUSH)
(Isaiah 43:3)

Syria Pays Tribute to Tiglath-pileser III

Tiglath-pileser III, king of Assyria, describes the war booty he obtained from Rezin, (or Rezon), the king of Syria. Rezin is also mentioned in Isaiah 7:1–7.

"I [Tiglath-pileser] received tribute from . . . Rezon of Damascus, . . . (to wit) gold, silver, tin, iron, elephant-hides, ivory, linen garments with multicolored trimmings, blue-dyed wool, purple-dyed wool, ebony-wood, . . . horses, mules, large and small cattle, (male) camels, female camels with their foals."

Source: James B. Pritchard, *Ancient Near Eastern Texts: Relating to the Old Testament,* 283.

Highlights of the Assyrian Empire during the Ministry of the Prophet Isaiah and Later

Tiglath-pileser III	**ca. 747–727 B.C.**
Consolidated control over Syria	743–738 B.C.
Countered Urartian incursion in the east	738–737 B.C.
Western campaigns subdued Syro-Ephraimite, anti-Assyrian coalition	734–732 B.C.
Occupied with Chaldean rebellion	731–729 B.C.
Shalmaneser V	**ca. 727–722 B.C.**
Shechem captured, Tyre beseiged	725 B.C.
Fall of Samaria	722 B.C.
Sargon II	**ca. 721–705 B.C.**
Elam blocked Sargon's approach to Babylon	721 B.C.
Western Coalition defeated	720 B.C.
Battled with Egypt	717–716 B.C.
Campaigned against Urartu	714 B.C.
Subdued western revolt by Ashdod and Judah	712 B.C.
Campaigned against Merodach-baladan in Babylon	710–704 B.C.
Sennacherib	**704–681 B.C.**
Merodach-baladan chased from the throne in Babylon	703 B.C.
Seige of Babylon	689 B.C.
Esarhaddon	**681–669 B.C.**
Babylon is rebuilt and control over the west is firm	676 B.C.
Control extended over Egypt	675–670 B.C.
Assurbanipal	**669–630 B.C.**
Fall of Thebes	663 B.C.
Aided Lydians against Cimmerians in Asia Minor, victory over Elamites	653 B.C.
Egypt breaks free with help of Lydians	651 B.C.
Rebellion in Babylon led by brother, Shamash-shun-ukin	650–648 B.C.
Devastated Elam	645 B.C.
Fall of Nineveh to Medes and Babylonians	612 B.C.

And it shall come to pass in that day, that every place shall be, where there were a thousand vines at a thousand silverlings, it shall even be for briers and thorns. . . . And on all hills that shall be digged with the mattock, there shall not come thither the fear of briers and thorns: but it shall be for the sending forth of oxen, and for the treading of lesser cattle.

This verse is part of Isaiah's prophecy regarding the impending Assyrian warfare against the kingdom of Judah (Isaiah 7:17–25). Because of the desolation of warfare, the vineyards would become neglected and overrun with thorns and briers (vv. 23–24). The farmlands that had once been cultivated, "digged with the mattock," would also be abandoned and become a pastureland for cattle and sheep (v. 25).

Isaiah prophesies that the fruits of the land would be lost with Assyria's invasion. The richest vines would become worthless, and briers and thorns would be found in place of vineyards.

Above: A large vineyard located between Jerusalem and Hebron. Because of rich soil and suitable climate, vineyards were common in the Holy Land. It is perhaps because of this commonality that many prophets have referred to vineyards in metaphors and parables.

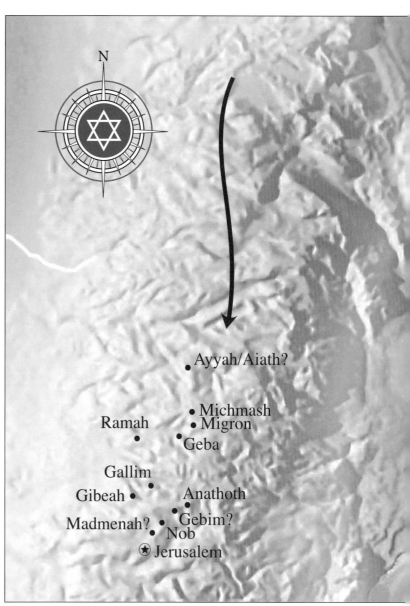

Assyria Marches to Jerusalem (Isaiah 10:28–32)
Arrow indicates possible route of Assyrian army.

Above: The Pool of Siloam of New Testament times is thought to be the same as the "waters of Shiloah" mentioned by Isaiah. The pool receives its waters from the Gihon Spring that flows through Hezekiah's Tunnel.

ISAIAH 8:6–7

Forasmuch as this people refuseth the waters of Shiloah that go softly, and rejoice in Rezin and Remaliah's son; Now therefore, behold, the Lord bringeth up upon them the waters of the river, strong and many, even the king of Assyria.

Isaiah describes and then contrasts two forms of waters, the "waters of Shiloah" and "the waters of the river." The soft, rolling waters of Shiloah flow near the Temple Mount in Jerusalem. They are controlled and inviting and bring life to those who drink them.

The waters of Shiloah represent Jesus, the King of Heaven, who is likened to the fountain of righteousness (Psalm 36:8–9; 1 Nephi 2:9; Ether 12:28).

The waters of the river represent the king of Assyria, who leads his great, destructive armies "like a flood" to "cover the earth" and "destroy the city and the inhabitants thereof" (Jeremiah 46:8).

Because the inhabitants of Judah rejected Jesus, the Lord sent against them the king of Assyria, or the strong and mighty waters of the river that would overflow its banks and cover the entire land with destruction.

Tiglath-pileser III's Flood Metaphor

According to one Assyrian royal inscription, Tiglath-pileser III (ca. 747–727 B.C.), king of Assyria, conquered hundreds of towns in ancient Syria. He compared this destruction to a sweeping flood. This flood metaphor is remarkably similar to a metaphor in Isaiah, also comparing the king of Assyria to a flood. The Lord promised that he would bring upon Syria and Israel "the waters of the river, strong and many, even the king of Assyria, and all his glory: and he shall come up over all his channels, and go over all his banks" (Isaiah 8:7).

Tiglath-pileser III describes it this way: "592 towns . . . of the 16 districts of the country of Damascus [Syria] I destroyed (making them look) like hills of (ruined cities over which) the flood (had swept)."

Source: James B. Pritchard, *Ancient Near Eastern Texts: Relating to the Old Testament,* 283.

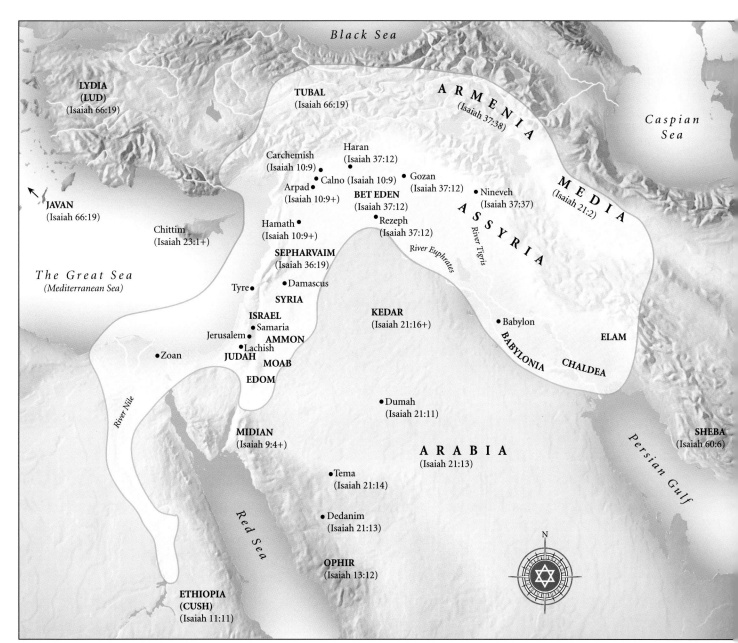

The Assyrian Empire, 9th to 7th Centuries B.C.

Assyrian Warfare

Assyrian kings launched multiple campaigns against kingdoms and peoples during Isaiah's lifetime. The Assyrian armies were equipped and disciplined to battle against fortified cities and villages as well as opposing armies on open terrain. The formal order of their army included the king and his officers who directed the chariotry, spearmen, slingsmen, cavalry, and archers. These illustrations are based on Assyrian relief carvings.

ISAIAH 10:5–6

O Assyrian, the rod of mine anger, and the staff in their hand is mine indignation. I will send him against an hypocritical nation, and against the people of my wrath will I give him a charge, to take the spoil, and to take the prey, and to tread them down like the mire of the streets.

To fulfill his divine purposes, the Lord sends Assyria's wicked king and his armies to war against Israel. The Lord is actively engaged in this process. "I will send him," he says. The Lord controls all nations and their armies. "Do I not hold the destinies of all the armies of the nations of the earth?" he asks (D&C 117:6).

The Lord uses the wicked to destroy a people who have forsaken the covenant and committed spiritual adultery by worshiping foreign gods. Assyria represents the Lord's rod of anger, which is used to punish the apostate Israelites. They had apostatized from the truth and were the "people of [God's] wrath." Assyria's army would trample and tread Israel's wicked in the deep mud, or mire.

ISAIAH 10:14

And my hand hath found as a nest the riches of the people: and as one gathereth eggs that are left, have I gathered all the earth; and there was none that moved the wing, or opened the mouth, or peeped.

This prophecy pertains to Assyria's conquest of ancient Israel (Isaiah 10:5–19). Israel is compared to a bird's nest, eggs, wings, and call. (See 3 Nephi 10:4–6; D&C 10:65; 29:1–2 for other examples of bird symbolism.) The eggs in the nest represent Israel's riches, which Assyria has raided. Israel's inability to move its wings or to make a peep signifies that it, like a little chick, is helpless before Assyria's ravening armies.

Above: Mire on the pathways of the Biblical Zoo, Jerusalem. Many streets in the biblical period lacked asphalt, cement, or even paving stones. They became deep mud, or mire, during the rainy season, January through March.

Above: Nest with eggs, near Kibbutz Eilon. Eggs were a valuable food source to the ancients.

Shall the axe boast itself against him that heweth therewith? Or shall the saw magnify itself against him that shaketh it?

To fulfill his divine purposes, the Lord sent Assyria's wicked king and his armies to war against Israel. Assyria became the ax and saw in the Lord's hand, used to cut down the apostate Israelites, namely, those who had forsaken the covenant and committed spiritual adultery by worshiping foreign deities. However, Assyria and its king were proud enough to believe that they were greater than God, not realizing they were really tools in God's hand.

Above: An ax leaning against a threshing sledge, Qatzrin, an ancient village from the talmudic period (ca. A.D. 200–500). Axes were common tools used anciently for trimming or felling trees, clearing heavy brush, or quarrying stone. Similar to its modern counterpart, the ax had a wooden handle with an iron head.

Above: A saw leaning on a post near a home, Qatzrin. The saw served in biblical times to cut both wood and stone. Blades were usually made of bronze or iron.

Tools Mentioned by Isaiah

anvil	41:7
axe	10:15
fan	30:24; 41:16
hammer(s)	41:7
instrument(s)	28:27; 41:15
plowshares	2:4
pruninghooks	2:9; 18:5
saw	10:15
shovel	30:24
threshing instrument	28:27
tongs	6:6; 44:12
yoke	10:27

ISAIAH 14:22–23

For I will rise up . . . and cut off from Babylon the name, and remnant, and son, and nephew, saith the Lord. I will also make it a possession for the bittern, and pools of water: and I will sweep it with the [broom] of destruction, saith the Lord of hosts.

Isaiah prophesies that God would put an end to Babylon, the great city of ancient Babylonia known for its huge walls, celebrated gardens and parks, and beautiful temples. Babylon's destruction would be so great that both "son" and "nephew"—those who would produce additional generations to inhabit Babylon—would be destroyed.

Isaiah's words were fulfilled in 539 B.C. when Cyrus, king of Persia, defeated Babylon together with its evil rulers and residents. How complete was Babylon's destruction? The Lord said, "I will sweep it with the broom of destruction." Just as one sweeps a house to eliminate dust and dirt, so God swept Babylon of its foulness so that nothing, not even dust, remained. Its temples and gardens are gone, and Babylon now stands in ruins, a testimony that Isaiah's words were fulfilled.

Babylon is a perfect example of an evil place that was destroyed by the power of God. As such, Babylon is a type and a shadow of the wicked world that will be destroyed by God's power in the last days (D&C 1:16).

Above: Broom with other household items, Qatzrin.

The Babylonian Empire, 605 to 538 B.C.

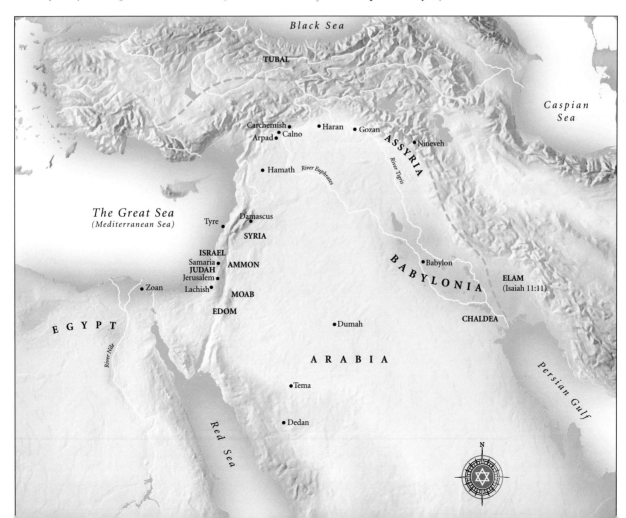

Uncommon Expressions from the King James Version of Isaiah

The "+"sign indicates the expression occurs more than once.

afar off = far away (23:7+)
aforetime = formerly (52:4)
ancients = elders (3:14+)
angle = hook (19:8)
art = are (14:8+)
astonied = astonished (52:14)
away with = endure (1:13+)
barren = unable to have children (54:1)
beforetime = previously (41:26)
beget/begettest = sire, give birth to (39:7)
beseech = implore (38:3+)
besom = broom (14:23)
bestead = distressed (8:21)
bestowed = granted (63:7)
betwixt = between (5:3)
bewail = lament (16:9)
bewray = betray (16:3)
bonnets = covering for the head (3:20)
brambles = thistles (34:13)
bulwarks = fortifications (26:1)
bunch = hump of a camel (30:6)
carbuncles = precious stones (54:12)
carriages = baggage, gear (10:28+)
cauls = headbands (3:18)
churl = knave (40:2+)
clave = split (48:21)
cockatrice = venomous serpent (11:8+)
compass = encircle (50:11+)
consolations = comfort (66:11)
consumption = destruction (28:22+)
contemned = despised (16:14)
cormorant = large water fowl (34:11)
corn = grain (17:5+)
crisping pins = instruments for curling hair (3:22)

cunning artificer = magician (3:3)
cunning workman = skillful craftsman (40:20)
dandled = bounced (66:12)
delectable = beloved (44:9)
digged = cultivated (7:25)
dimness = dark affliction (8:22+)
disannul = cancel (14:27)
discomfited = enslaved (31:8)
divorcement = divorce (50:1)
doctrine = precept, instruction (28:9+)
doleful = howling (13:21)
doth = does (1:3+)
dragons = jackals or wild dogs (13:22+)
dregs = remains (51:17+)
dromedaries = one-humped camels (60:6)
dryshod = dry footed (11:15)
dunghill = heap of dung or refuse (25:10)
durable clothing = fine clothing (23:18)
ear the ground = plow the ground (30:24)
enchantments = spells (47:9+)
eveningtide = evening (17:14)
exactors = taskmasters (60:17)
fainthearted = timid (7:4)
fatness = fullness of flesh (17:4+)
feller = tree-cutter (14:8)
firebrands = smoldering sticks (7:4)
fitches = dill (28:25+)
flagons = jars (22:24)
fro = from (24:20+)
frowardly = turning away (57:17)
fuller = launderer (7:3+)
gin = trap, snare (8:14)
girdle = belt, sash (3:24+)
grievous = bitter, difficult (15:4)

Right: An acacia tree is called a "shittah" in the King James Version of Isaiah.

harvestman = reaper (17:5)

hast = have (2:6+)

hasten = accelerate (5:19)

hasting = hurrying (16:5)

hath = has (1:2+)

henceforth = from this time forth (52:1+)

hireling = hired worker (16:14+)

hither = here (57:3)

ho = a call to stop or rally (55:1)

hoar hairs = white or gray hairs (46:4)

impoverished = poor, weak (40:20)

laden = burdened (1:4)

latchet = thong used to fasten a shoe (5:27)

lees = to the last drop (25:6)

lest = for fear that (6:10+)

lo = behold (6:7+)

loaden = weighted (46:1)

lovingkindnesses = the active love of God for His creatures (63:7)

mantles = cloaks (3:22)

mart = marketplace (23:3)

mattock = garden hoe (7:25)

mean = ordinary (2:9+)

meat = food (62:8+)

merryhearted = joyful (24:7)

mine own = my (37:35)

mirth = happiness (24:8+)

mollified = softened (1:6)

mufflers = wraps or scarves (3:19)

mustereth = gather, appoint (13:4)

nettles = a plant that grows on waste ground and is noted for its stinging properties (34:13)

nought = nothing (8:10+)

outmost = situated farthest out (17:6)

overpast = passed over (26:20)

plaister = anoint, smear (38:21)

plowman = a man who guides a plow, farm laborer (28:24)

polluted = impure (47:6+)

potsherd = broken piece of pottery (45:9)

prognosticators = foretellers (47:13)

putrifying = rotting (1:6)

reckoned = considered (38:13)

rent = torn (36:22+)

replenished = filled, supplied (2:6+)

reproach = disgrace, shame (4:1+)

rereward = rearguard (52:12+)

revilings = abusive language (51:7)

rie = grain (rye) (28:25)

rod = a straight, slender shoot growing from a tree or bush (11:1+)

roe = deer (13:14)

rottenness = decay (5:24)

ruinous heaps = heaps and ruins (37:26)

rushes = cattails (35:7)

satyrs = wild goats (13:21+)

shalt = shall (1:18+)

shew = show (43:9+)

shittah = acacia (41:19)

silverlings = pieces of silver (7:23)

sodering = soldering (41:7)

softly = slowly, gently (8:6+)

soothsayers = sorcerers (2:6)

spoiler = destroyer (16:4+)

stomacher = robe (3:24)

stouthearted = hardhearted (46:12)

stoutness = pride, haughtiness (9:9)

straight = direct (40:3+)

strange slips = foreign cuts for grafting (17:10+)

substance = potential life (6:13+)

sucking child = nursing child (11:8+)

(in) sunder = in pieces (27:9+)

tabret(s) = drums or tambourines (24:8+)

tacklings = riggings of a ship (33:23)

tarry = wait (46:13)

teil tree = oak or elm tree (6:13)

thence = from that place (52:11+)

thereon = on (30:12+)

thereto = to that or to it (44:15)

thine = yours (6:7+)

thither = towards that place (7:25+)

tin = dross (1:25)

tires = a covering, dress, or ornament for a woman's head (3:18)

tow = tinder (1:31+)

traffickers = merchants (23:8)

travaileth = give birth (13:8+)

trodden = trampled (14:19+)

twain = two (6:2)

unicorns = wild oxen? (34:7)

uphold = support (41:10+)

utterly = totally (2:18+)

uttermost = outermost (7:18+)

vail = veil (25:7)

vexation = anguish (9:1+)

villany = obscenity (32:6)

viol = lyre (5:12)

visage = appearance, face (52:14)

wast = were (12:1+)

waster = destroyer (54:16)

wasting = desolation (59:7+)

wax = grow (29:22+)

wayfaring = journeying (33:8+)

whence = from what place (30:6+)

whereas = since (37:21+)

whereto = for which (55:11)

wherewith = with which (28:12+)

whither = where (20:6)

wholly = completely (22:1)

wilt = will (38:12+)

wimples = cloth head coverings or cloaks (3:22)

winefat = winepress (63:2)

withal = therewith (30:14+)

wither = dry up (19:6+)

wroth = angry (47:6+)

wrought = performed (26:12+)

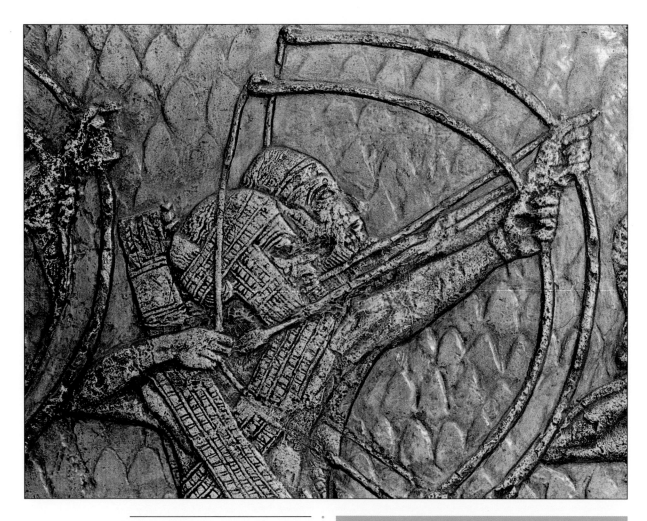

Above: Two Assyrian archers dressed in armor, with bent bows, Assyrian palace relief, Nineveh. The bows in the picture are typical of those used by warriors at the time of Isaiah. Assyrian archers, with their superior weapons, caused great fear in the hearts of the inhabitants of ancient Israel. Their bows consisted of laminated wood with strings made of stretched, dried sheep gut. Their arrows had wooden shafts, metal heads, and three or four vanes.

Military Terms

archers	21:17; 22:3
army/armies	36:2; 43:17
captain	3:3; 36:9
horsemen	21:7, 9
host(s)	13:4; 24:21
officers	60:17
standardbearer	10:18
troop	65:11
warrior	9:5
watchman/men	21:6, 11

ISAIAH 21:15

For they fled from the swords, from the drawn sword, and from the bent bow, and from the grievousness of war.

The setting of Isaiah 21:15 is Tema, an oasis and important caravan stop on an ancient trade route on the Arabian peninsula. It was approximately two hundred fifty miles southeast of Aqaba. Isaiah speaks concerning the inhabitants of Tema who fled from a fierce battle that destroyed much of Tema's population. Their flight from both "drawn sword" and "bent bow" suggests they escaped from the heat of the battle.

The bow was a weapon used among many peoples in antiquity. Isaiah referred to the bow in several of his prophecies (Isaiah 5:28; 7:24; 13:18; 41:2; 66:19). In almost every instance, the bow alludes to war.

The burden of Tyre . . . Be still, ye inhabitants of the isle; thou whom the merchants of Zidon, that pass over the sea, have replenished. And by great waters the seed of Sihor, the harvest of the river, is her revenue; and she is a [market place] of nations.

Tyre and Zidon (sometimes spelled Sidon) were famous Phoenician cities noted for their commerce, great wealth, and materialism. Tyre was so well-known by Mediterranean trading nations that it was called a mart, or market place, of nations. Its traders and merchants were so celebrated that they were equated with the "princes" and the "honorable of the earth" (Isaiah 23:8).

Zidon's merchants carried corn, dyed cloth, grain, wine, metal, horses, wood, and oil as they voyaged on the seas. Tyre was supported, or replenished, by Zidon's trading. The "seed of Sihor" refers to the grain produced near Sihor, and the "harvest of the river" likely refers to the great fishing industry in both Tyre and Zidon.

The Lord spoke against Tyre and its inhabitants, decrying its pride by calling it a harlot. He also warned its inhabitants to repent, or the city would become desolate. Tyre's inhabitants did not listen to the prophet and were destroyed. (vv. 16–18)

Like many modern cities, the primary interests of the inhabitants of Tyre lie in obtaining material wealth. If modern cities' inhabitants are proud, glory in wickedness, and sell themselves to the ways of the world—they will share Tyre's fate. They will be destroyed when the Lord returns to the earth with great glory. Tyre, then, serves as a warning of the pitfalls of pride and materialism.

Above: Bags of grain, lentils, and spices at a market in Akko. The market, frequently located near the village or city gate, was an important gathering place for tradesmen, countrymen, and community inhabitants. Children played games, and adults met there. Merchants and traders brought their wares, and farmers carried their produce to the market.

Below: Various goods and produce are sold at the market at Damascus Gate, Jerusalem. Perhaps a similar scene existed at the time of Isaiah.

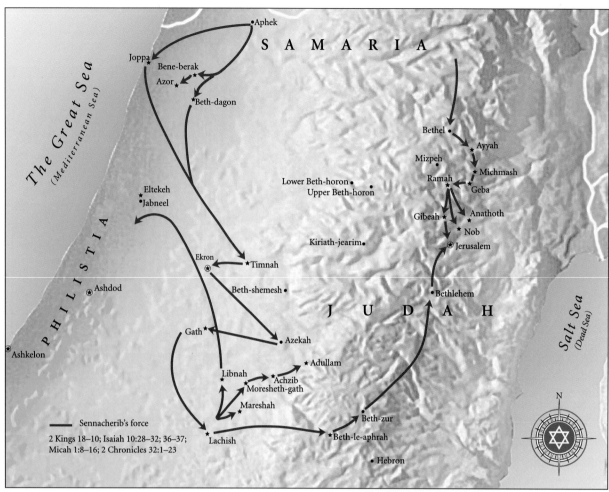

The Campaign of Sennacherib in Philistia and Judah, 701 B.C.
Adapted from *Macmillan Bible Atlas,* 154

Right: Assyrians besiege Lachish, a fortified city in the kingdom of Judah, Assyrian palace relief, Nineveh. Assyria became a world power partly because of its sophisticated war vehicles and machinery. Note the ram that batters the tower of Lachish. Judean soldiers atop the tower attempt to defend their city, which would soon fall into the hands of the Assyrians.

ISAIAH 36:1

Now it came to pass in the fourteenth year of king Hezekiah, that Sennacherib king of Assyria came up against all the defenced cities of Judah, and took them.

While Hezekiah served as king over Judah, Sennacherib, the king of Assyria (704–681 B.C.), and his armies captured most of the fortified cities of Judah. This occurred during the "fourteenth year of king Hezekiah," or approximately 701 B.C., the later years of Isaiah's ministry. After capturing most of the cities, Sennacherib sent his armies to Jerusalem to demand tribute and to inform Judah of the terms of surrender, which included the peoples' deportation (Isaiah 36:2, 8, 16–17).

Top right: The remains of Lachish, a city of Judah destroyed by the Assyrians. The heaps of stones from ruined structures and fallen walls shown in the photograph accord with Isaiah's words that Assyria would overthrow the cities of Judah.

Right: A palace relief at Nineveh depicts King Sennacherib of Assyria seated on his elaborately decorated throne, attended by two servants holding fly whisks. Sennacherib's general and a delegation of soldiers stand before him. A cuneiform caption above the scene states, "Sennacherib, King of the World, King of Assyria, sat on a throne; the booty from Lachish was paraded before him."

Scriptural Parallels in Isaiah, 2 Kings, and 2 Chronicles

Subject	Isaiah	2 Kings	2 Chronicles
Sennacherib and the Assyrian armies invade Judah	36:2–22	18:17–37	32:9–17
Hezekiah prays and the Lord responds	37:1–38	19:1–37	32:20–21
Hezekiah's psalm	38:1–22	20:1–11	32:24–26
Isaiah's prophecy of Babylonian captivity	39:1–8	20:12–19	32:31

Above: Grass on the housetops, Qatzrin, an ancient village from the talmudic period (ca. A.D. 200–500). Ancient Israelite homes generally had two to four rooms and were one or two stories high, depending upon the wealth of the owner. Some homes were built of stone, others of adobe. The roofs were flat, constructed of wood beams covered with brush and packed mud. Grass sometimes grew on the roof.

Below: Clay that has been trampled in the backroom of a pottery factory near Patriarch's Tomb, Hebron. Before sculpting clay, a potter adds straw, sand, or water to it to achieve proper consistency. He then works the clay by hand or treads on it to mix it and remove air bubbles.

ISAIAH 37:27

Therefore their inhabitants were of small power, they were dismayed and confounded: they were as the grass of the field, and as the green herb, as the grass on the housetops, and as corn blasted before it be grown up.

The great Assyrian nation, with its fierce and well-disciplined armies, destroyed other equally evil nations. During Isaiah's ministry, Assyria laid waste many nations, including the northern kingdom of Israel. The inhabitants of these conquered nations were powerless before the Assyrian army, as weak as fragile herbs before the scorching desert wind or as the grass on the housetops that cannot find root (Psalms 37:2; 90:5–6; Isaiah 40:6–8).

This scenario of Assyria at war anticipates the warring nations of the latter days, who will contend for land, power, and riches. They will thirst for blood. But as Assyria, its leaders, and its armies were destroyed according to God's plan, so also will the warring nations of the last days be annihilated at the second coming. Meanwhile, a righteous remnant of Israel will be saved as they worship in temples and obey God's words.

ISAIAH 41:25

He shall come upon princes as upon mortar, and as the potter treadeth clay.

This passage refers to King Cyrus of Persia, whom the Lord raised up to be a conqueror. Cyrus's military campaigns were so successful that he conquered the Medes, Lydians, and Babylonians and their dynasties of powerful princes and kings. Cyrus trod on kings and princes as easily as a potter treads on his clay to prepare it for his work.

This passage also refers to Jesus Christ. In ancient days, Israel was in bondage to an earthly conqueror, Babylon, but God called up Cyrus to deliver Israel. Today all people are in bondage, but their enslavement is to sin, false tradition, and death. In his great power, God has sent a deliverer in Jesus Christ. The Savior has the power to set people free spiritually if they will turn to him and accept his atonement. But to receive his blessing, they must be willing to submit to him, even as the clay does to the potter.

ISAIAH 45:2

I will go before thee, and make the crooked places straight: I will break in pieces the gates of brass, and cut in sunder the bars of iron.

The end of Isaiah 44 and the beginning of Isaiah 45 speak of Cyrus, king of Persia, who is called the Lord's "shepherd" and "anointed." The Lord addresses Cyrus, although not yet born, calling him by name and appointing him to serve as a deliverer of captive Israel (Isaiah 45:1–2).

The Lord prepared the way for Cyrus to deliver ancient Israel, which was held captive by the Babylonians, by opening doors and making rough places smooth (vv. 1–2). In the same way, the Lord will open doors and prepare the way for his covenant people of the latter days to overcome sin. God exercised his power to break even the most imposing barriers—crooked places, gates of brass, and bars of iron—that stood in Cyrus's way. In a similar manner, God will exercise power to remove the barriers that prevent his followers from doing his will, if they will trust in him.

ISAIAH 47:2

Take the millstones, and grind meal: uncover thy locks, make bare the leg, uncover the thigh.

Isaiah describes the work of a female slave who uses a millstone to grind meal. She has to keep her hair from her face, as well as tie up her skirts to keep hair and clothing from hindering her work. This work of the female slave symbolizes the servitude into which Babylon, the wicked world, would be forced. It would be the end of a life of decadence.

Babylon was forced to serve its masters when it fell. The wicked serve their master, Satan. Satan promises the wicked a life of pleasure but delivers only bondage and pain. Only righteousness brings lasting rewards.

Above: Two leaved gates, Pater Noster Church, Jerusalem. Huge walls surrounded many biblical cities, and an elaborate system of gates facilitated the flow of traffic while protecting the city. One gate system, for example, had walls at right angles to the main walls, a small courtyard being formed between two gates. Great bars of iron secured the doors of the gates. Exposed to their enemies' arrows and spears, approaching armies would have to penetrate both gates to gain entrance to the city.

Below left: An ancient millstone used to grind grain, Bet Guvrin National Park.

Below right: An ancient millstone, covered with brush, on a trail south of Banias. Millstones were the most common tool for grinding grain in the ancient Near East. They operated on the basis of one stone rotating upon a second, crushing grain placed between the two.

WARNINGS TO THE WICKED

The wicked who lived during Isaiah's lifetime committed numerous sins. They ate inappropriate foods, sought the treasures of the world, partook of strong drinks, and made monuments to themselves. They were spiritually blind, prideful, and vain. They worshiped false gods and trusted in their own abilities rather than relying on God. Wicked people today commit the same sins. Isaiah's words warn the wicked—then and now—that unless they obey God, they will be smitten by their enemies.

Sheep forage for food, Shepherd's Fields, near Bethlehem.

Above: Fading leaves from an oak tree. The Hebrew *ela* (Isaiah 1:30) is better translated "terebinth" *(Pistacia atlantica)* rather than "oak." The terebinth took a prominent position in various Old Testament settings. Jacob hid idols under a terebinth (Genesis 35:4). Joshua set up a stone under a terebinth (Joshua 24:26). Absalom, David's son, caught his hair in one of the branches of a terebinth while riding upon a mule and remained helpless in the tree when Joab came upon him and murdered him (2 Samuel 18:9, 14).

ISAIAH 1:30

For ye shall be as an oak whose leaf fadeth, and as a garden that hath no water.

The two metaphors here, the oak and the garden, symbolize what will happen to the wicked. Because the wicked have chosen to worship idols that are associated with oaks and gardens, they will become, in a sense, what they have worshiped (Isaiah 1:29). They will be as valueless as an oak tree that is dying or diseased, "an oak whose leaf fadeth," or as unfruitful and worthless as "a garden that hath no water."

The oak tree that lacks water soon shrivels up and becomes kindling for fire. A dry garden is in a similar state. The wicked will be like kindling for the fire accompanying the second coming of Jesus that will burn all corruptible things. Spiritually, Jesus represents the living water (Isaiah 33:21; Jeremiah 2:13; 17:13; John 4:6–14). By partaking of this living water, the righteous will be spiritually quenched rather than desolate.

ISAIAH 5:11

Woe unto them that rise up early in the morning, that they may follow strong drink; that continue until night, till wine inflame them!

This passage indicates revelry and unholy merry-making among those who spend time in immoral entertainment. It warns all against making strong drink their passion. A passage from the Book of Mormon presents a prophecy that corresponds in some ways to this verse of Isaiah: "There shall be many which shall say: Eat, drink, and be merry, for tomorrow we die; and it shall be well with us" (2 Nephi 28:7). But these are "false and vain and foolish doctrines" (Isaiah 5:9).

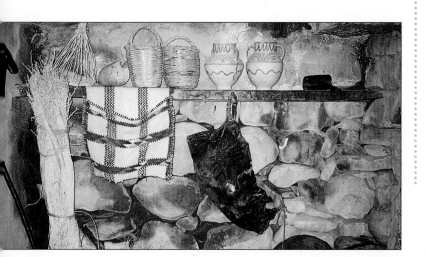

Above and right: A wineskin, probably made of goat skin, Qatzrin, an ancient village from the talmudic period (ca. A.D. 200–500). Wine was stored in earthenware jars or containers made from leather. Wine and strong drink were made during the Old Testament period and caused intoxication when abused.

ISAIAH 5:12

And the harp, and the viol, the [tambourine],
and pipe, and wine, are in their feasts: but they
regard not the work of the Lord, neither consider
the operation of his hands.

Above: Tambourine at the marketplace, Old City, Jerusalem. The tambourine mentioned in the Bible was a hand-held percussion instrument covered with a membrane. It was used to accompany singing and dancing at festive occasions.

Harps, tambourines, and other instruments were played in antiquity (Genesis 4:21; Psalm 137:2) and are mentioned in Isaiah's prophecies (Isaiah 5:12; 24:8). The King James Version of the Bible uses the word "tabret," which is usually translated "tambourine" in modern English Bibles.

Instruments were used in worship. They were also played at banquets and feasts where merrymakers partook of wine and strong drink and participated in revelries. Apparently, harlots played their harps as they wandered around the city attempting to attract attention (Isaiah 23:16).

Right: A man in biblical costume plays a harp. Many musical instruments, including the harp, are mentioned in the Bible. The harp was used in the temple and during various festivities. The harp was made of wood, perhaps cypress or almug, and its strings consisted of stretched and dried sheep gut.

Above: Cart at Neot Kedumim, a biblical landscape reserve. Carts were versatile vehicles that served Old Testament peoples for millennia. They generally had two or four spoked wheels. The carts were made of wood and were pulled by asses or other animals. Some carts were covered, others were open. The carts hauled produce, merchandise, and people.

Above: Gazelles, Biblical Zoo, Jerusalem. According to Mosaic law, the roe deer was a clean animal that could be eaten. It may have been a delicacy, as King Solomon made it part of the royal table (1 Kings 4:22–23). Many species of deer and antelope still inhabit Israel and may be seen in the upper Galilee region or Judean hills.

Woe unto them that draw iniquity with cords of vanity, and sin as it were with a cart rope.

This verse creates an image of a beast of burden, such as a donkey or ox, pulling a cart of goods. The beast represents a wicked person and the cart represents sin. The wicked are burdened with sins, which they drag behind them, just as a beast of burden hauls its load from place to place.

The verse also suggests that vanity is the key component from which the cords are made. Many commit sins and then drag them after themselves because of vanity and pride. Sin is sometimes as difficult to break as a thick rope that is strong enough to pull a cart, but it is possible to break sin with the help of Christ. The Lord says, "Come unto me, all ye that labour and are heavy laden, and I will give you rest" (Matthew 11:28).

ISAIAH 13:14

And it shall be as the chased roe and as a sheep that no man taketh up.

Isaiah compares deer and sheep in precarious situations to wicked people during the judgments of the last days. A "chased roe" is a hunted deer, and "sheep that no man taketh up" are vulnerable because their shepherds are absent. The imagery implies that the wicked will be like hunted deer. They will flee for their lives during a time of wars.

ISAIAH 22:15–16

Thus saith the Lord God of hosts, Go, get thee unto this treasurer, even unto Shebna . . . and say, what hast thou here? . . . that thou hast hewed thee out a sepulchre here, as he that heweth him out a sepulchre on high, and that graveth an habitation for himself in a rock?

Isaiah speaks of a historical character, Shebna, who was Isaiah's contemporary and likely acquainted with him. Shebna was an important and influential government official or treasurer who served in the court of Hezekiah, king of Judah (Isaiah 22:15; 37:2). Shebna, a proud, wealthy man, is rebuked by the Lord for his arrogance in building himself a monumental tomb.

Shebna apparently had prepared a sepulcher in a high and conspicuous place, a monument to himself for all to view. In doing so, he was setting himself up "on high." Therefore, Isaiah prophesies that a judgment will fall upon the treasurer's head. Shebna would lose his important position in the kingdom of Judah. He would be violently carried into captivity, his glory would become shame, and he would die in exile (vv. 17–19).

The location of Shebna's sepulcher is unknown, although some scholars place it with other tombs carved in rock in the valley of Kidron, east of Jerusalem. Shebna symbolizes all proud and arrogant people.

Above: Absalom's tomb, Kidron Valley (first century B.C.). Sepulchers were frequently hewn from rock cliffs in conspicuous places to honor the deceased who would be buried there. The sepulchers functioned primarily as monuments, and many sepulchers from antiquity still stand.

Left: Tombs of the priestly family Bene Hezir (ca. first century B.C.), overlooking the Kidron Valley.

Above: Karak Castle, Jordan, was built by the Crusaders in A.D. 1142. Once a great fortress, the castle is now in ruins.

Social Terms

beloved	5:1
brethren	66:5, 20
friend	41:8
handmaids	14:2
harlot	1:21; 23:15–16
lady	47:5, 7
lords	16:8; 26:13
maid	24:2
man/men	2:9, 11
mate	34:15–16
mistress	24:2
nobles	13:2; 34:12; 43:14
servant(s)	14:2; 20:3
virgin(s)	7:14; 23:4, 12; 37:22; 47:1; 62:5
woman/women	3:12; 4:1

ISAIAH 25:11–12

He shall bring down their pride together with the spoils of their hands. And the fortress of the high fort of thy walls shall he bring down, lay low, and bring to the ground, even to the dust.

Jehovah plays an active role in the events that will occur during the last days and at his second coming. This is set forth in Isaiah 25:6–12 and other passages. In verse 11, Isaiah prophesies that the Lord will bring down the pride of the wicked, along with the spoil, or the things they have gained through treacherous deeds. (See Proverbs 16:18 for another description of the fate of the proud.)

In verse 12, Isaiah prophesies that the fortresses of the wicked—symbolic of reliance on military might, the arm of flesh, and worldly powers—will be destroyed. To emphasize the completeness of their destruction, Isaiah uses repetitive language: "bring down," "lay low," "bring down to the ground," and "to the dust."

ISAIAH 28:20

For the bed is shorter than that a man can stretch himself on it: and the covering narrower than that he can wrap himself in it.

This verse pertains to Isaiah's prophecy that the Assyrian army would scourge the southern kingdom of Judah (Isaiah 28:14–22). This scourge would come because of Judah's wicked practices and failure to recognize that Jehovah is God and King. The scourge would come day and night, and when the inhabitants heard of it, they would be visibly frightened.

Isaiah compares the fear of Judah's inhabitants to one who lies in his bed but cannot find comfort. In the same way that a small bed is too short for a tall person or a small blanket does not adequately cover an adult, the wicked would not find adequate calm or protection from the Assyrian scourge.

Below: Bed at Qatzrin, an ancient village from the talmudic period (ca. A.D. 200–500).

Below: The remains of the castle at Ajloun, Jordan, built by Azz Al Din Ausama in A.D. 1184–85.

ISAIAH 46:1

Bel boweth down, Nebo stoopeth, their idols were upon the beasts, and upon the cattle: your carriages were heavy loaden; they are a burden to the weary beast.

The term "idols" refers both to heathen deities constructed of wood, stone, or other materials and to more abstract things that people worship. People may become excessively devoted to wealth, the honor of men, or worldly things. Isaiah also speaks of idols in Isaiah 2:8, 18, 20; 10:10–11; 19:1, 3; and 31:7. The law of Moses speaks clearly against the creation and worship of idols (Exodus 20:3–4).

In the belief system of the Babylonians, Bel and Nebo were two chief gods. Bel was the father of all other gods. Nebo was the god of learning and wisdom. Idols representing these gods had no power to help themselves against the encroachments of enemies. They were carried away on the backs of beasts into captivity and could not prevent it (Isaiah 46:1–2). The idols were equally powerless to help the people who worshiped them.

In contrast to the idols, Jehovah carries his people "from the womb," and he continues to carry them "even to [their] old age" (vv. 3–4). While the idols have no power to deliver even themselves, Jehovah delivers his people (vv. 2, 4). The idol worshipers may spend a fortune on their images, but idols cannot help them in their time of "trouble" (vv. 6–7).

Left: A gold idol, excavated at Megiddo. Idol worshiping was a common practice among ancient Near Eastern religions. Modern scholars are not certain how the ancients imagined that their deities could be present in the statues and images. At times the worshipers bathed, clothed, and presented food to the statues. In any case, God's prophets, including Isaiah, prohibited idol worship.

ISAIAH 46:6

They lavish gold out of the bag, and weigh silver in the balance, and they hire a goldsmith; and he maketh it a god: they fall down, yea, they worship.

Idol worshipers from biblical times would sometimes hire a smith to make a god from gold or silver. They would pray to it and show reverence to it. Occasionally, priests and worshipers built temples to house their idols and offered them sacrifices.

Despite the attention paid to idols, and though they are often made of precious materials, they still have no power (Isaiah 44:15–17). They cannot "answer, nor save him out of his trouble" (Isaiah 46:7).

ISAIAH 50:11

Behold, all ye that kindle a fire, that compass yourselves about with sparks: walk in the light of your fire, and in the sparks that ye have kindled. This shall ye have of mine hand; ye shall lie down in sorrow.

People who kindle and walk in the light of their own fire are those who walk in their own way. They act according to their own will, rather than according to the will and direction of the Lord. They seek to be spiritually self-sufficient, relying on themselves instead of on God. They attempt to create their own light, but their efforts produce no more than short-lived sparks compared to the everlasting bright light that comes from God. Sadly, they deny themselves his greater light. Such will eventually be judged by the Lord, resulting in sorrow.

Above: Idol, on a beast. Artisans and goldsmiths carefully crafted small idols to be used in homes. Idols or household deities were regularly worshiped, and sacrifices and offerings were presented to them. Members of the house of Israel, at times, also practiced idol worship, although God's prophets warned against idolatry.

Isaiah describes the manner in which carpenters made household idols from logs: "The carpenter stretcheth out his rule: he marketh it out with a line; he fitteth it with planes, and he marketh it out with the compass, and maketh it after the figure of a man, according to the beauty of a man; that it may remain in the house" (Isaiah 44:13).

Right: Fire and smoke, on the road between Bet Guvrin National Park and Jerusalem. Fire served the ancients in many ways. It was used for cooking, heating, lighting, and making pottery and metal products.

Above: Men stand guard on the wall above Damascus Gate, Jerusalem. Suleiman built the wall in A.D. 1535.

ISAIAH 56:10

His watchmen are blind: they are all ignorant, they are all dumb dogs, they cannot bark; sleeping, lying down, loving to slumber.

Watchmen are those, particularly leaders, who know the gospel and are charged to protect it from apostasy (Ezekiel 3:17). In this passage, the watchmen themselves have become apostates. Isaiah refers to these negligent watchmen as ineffectual dogs and shepherds. Like watchdogs who have become lazy, blind, and inept, or like shepherds who are no longer able to recognize the enemy, these watchmen have left off caring for their flock. They have turned instead to caring for their own needs and desires. (See Ezekiel 34:1–28 for a detailed description of indolent shepherds and the Lord's reaction to them.)

The Lord's criticism of these unrighteous leaders is scathing. He calls them blind watchmen, "ignorant," "dumb dogs," "greedy dogs," and "shepherds that cannot understand" (Isaiah 56:10–11). Besides describing Israel's religious leaders in ancient times, this prophecy may also refer to leaders of modern-day apostate religions (2 Nephi 28:3–9; Mormon 8:31–33, 37–39).

ISAIAH 57:20

The wicked are like the troubled sea, when it cannot rest, whose waters cast up mire and dirt.

The Lord promises peace to the righteous. "Peace, peace to him that is far off, and to him that is near, saith the Lord; and I will heal him" (Isaiah 57:19). The wicked do not have this promise. In fact, the Lord says, "There is no peace, saith my God, to the wicked" (v. 21). Isaiah uses the image of a troubled sea to describe the condition of the wicked. He indicates that their life is similar to the mire and dirt that is cast up by stormy waters.

Left: The Mediterranean Sea, near Caesarea. Did Isaiah travel from Jerusalem to one of the great seas that border the Holy Land—the Mediterranean Sea, the Dead Sea, or the Sea of Galilee—and personally observe waves washing upon the shore? It is very likely, although the book of Isaiah tells the reader very little about Isaiah's private life.

ISAIAH 59:10

We grope for the wall like the blind, and we grope as if we had no eyes: we stumble at noonday as in the night.

Those who have turned from the light, at least in their hearts, are unable to find their way through life. They are like the blind, or like those who have no eyes at all. Consequently, night and noon are the same to them. Spiritual brightness and darkness are indistinguishable to those who have no spiritual eyes. This is the fulfillment of a curse pronounced on the wicked by the Lord (Deuteronomy 28:28–29). The Lord has power to heal this spiritual blindness if those who suffer will repent and return unto him.

ISAIAH 59:11

We roar all like bears, and mourn sore like doves: we look for judgment, but there is none; for salvation, but it is far off from us.

Ancient Israel's anguished laments are sometimes loud like the angry roaring or growling of bears. Sometimes they are soft and subdued, like the sad moaning of doves. Why does Israel, or any person, suffer such distress? Anguish often comes because of wickedness and its fruits. Even when they inflict themselves, the wicked become angry at the troubles of sin. The passage in Isaiah 59:12–13 speaks concerning Israel's "transgressions," "sins," "iniquities," "transgressing," "lying," "departing away from our God," "speaking oppression," "revolt," and "falsehood."

Above: Bear, Biblical Zoo, Jerusalem. Bears are used as symbols in many passages of scripture, especially in the writings of Daniel and John. The great mammal once roamed the forests of the Holy Land.

Discarded vessels, Cana. The vessels shown in the photograph are not ancient, but they illustrate the types of jars, bowls, pots, and containers that may have existed in the days of Isaiah.

ISAIAH 65:4

... which remain among the graves, and lodge in the monuments, which eat swine's flesh, and broth of abominable things is in their vessels.

In Isaiah 65:2–5, the Lord lists transgressions of his ancient covenant people: they do not walk in God's ways, their works are evil, they walk after their own thoughts, they provoke God to anger, they sacrifice in gardens, they burn incense on altars of brick, they lodge in cemeteries, they eat the flesh of swine, they pollute their vessels, and they say to others, "I am holier than thou."

Many of their transgressions represent clear violations of the laws God gave through Moses. For example, the statement "remain among the graves, and lodge in the monuments" may refer to an effort to communicate with the spirits of the dead, an action forbidden by Mosaic law (Leviticus 19:31; Deuteronomy 18:10–12; Isaiah 8:19). The statement "eat swine's flesh, and broth of abominable things" describes another violation of Mosaic law (Leviticus 11:7–8; Deuteronomy 14:7–8). The people were eating unclean animals or unclean sacrificial flesh (Leviticus 7:18; 19:7). And the statement "broth of abominable things is in their vessels" refers to people making their pots, pans, and dishes unclean by eating foods forbidden by the Lord.

Near Eastern Kings during the Ministry of Isaiah

Kings of Assyria

Tiglath-pileser III	ca. 747–727 B.C.
Shalmaneser V	ca. 727–722 B.C.
Sargon II	ca. 721–705 B.C.
Sennacherib	704–681 B.C.

Kings of Moab

Mesha	Days of Omri

Kings of Egypt

Sheshonk IV	?–727 B.C.
Osorkon IV	727–715 B.C.
Shabako	716–702 B.C.
Shebitku	702–690 B.C.

Kings of Israel

Menahem	ca. 747–742 B.C.
Pekahiah	ca. 742–740 B.C.
Pekah	ca. 740–731 B.C.
Hoshea	ca. 731–722 B.C.

Kings of Judah

Uzziah	ca. 767–739 B.C.
Jotham	ca. 739–734 B.C.
Ahaz	ca. 734–728 B.C.
Hezekiah	ca. 728–698 B.C.
Manasseh	ca. 698–642 B.C.

Above: A large cemetery, Mount of Olives, Jerusalem.

Blessings and Duties of the Righteous

One of Isaiah's major themes is that God requires righteousness of his people. The prophet admonishes the people to "prepare," "fast," "gather," and be clean. Parallel to these instructions are the blessings that come to those who obey: they will have "peace . . . as a river," they will "not hunger or thirst," and "the Lord shall guide" them.

Below Banias Falls. This river feeds into the Jordan.

Wash you, make you clean; put away the evil of your doings from before mine eyes; cease to do evil.

The term "wash" may refer to members of the priesthood washing their hands and feet with water before entering the temple. This was practiced in biblical times (Exodus 29:4). It also points to baptism, which is a ritual cleansing from sins and transgressions (Joseph Fielding Smith, *Answers to Gospel Questions*, 1:51). Ultimately, washing with water represents symbolic washing with the blood of Christ to become spiritually clean.

Above: Laver from a model of Solomon's temple. Water played an important role in the law of Moses in the ceremonial washing of members of the priesthood (Exodus 29:4; Numbers 8:7). A huge brass laver in the temple precinct was a visible reminder of the cleansing that had to take place before the temple service began. The laver sat on the backs of twelve oxen—three facing east, three facing west, three facing south, and three facing north.

Below: The Dan River, near Tel Dan, flows toward the Sea of Galilee.

For thou hast made of a city an heap; of a defenced city a ruin: a palace of strangers to be no city; it shall never be built.

Those who survive the judgments and the destructions upon the earth, as set forth in Isaiah 24, will praise the Lord, perhaps in prayer or song. Isaiah provides the words of a hymn of praise in Isaiah 25:1–5. The hymn includes words that bring Isaiah's readers great comfort: Jehovah is Israel's "strength" and "refuge from the storm." He is the "shadow from the heat." He is always there when his children need him, whether for spiritual protection or physical safety. The hymn begins:

> O Lord, thou art my God;
> I will exalt thee,
> I will praise thy name;
> for thou hast done wonderful things;
> thy counsels of old are faithfulness and truth. (v. 1)

Then follow expressions that speak of God making a city into a "heap" and a "ruin."

> For thou hast made of a city an heap;
> of a defenced city a ruin:
> a palace of strangers to be no city;
> it shall never be built. (v. 2)

"City" here refers to all cities wherein wickedness reigns. It appears in the singular form, perhaps recalling the ancient city of Babylon, which represents worldliness (D&C 1:16). The righteous will praise God's name and the "wonderful things" he has done, including destroying Babylon or cities that are like Babylon in their wickedness.

Above and below: The palace of Ahab, located in Samaria, is here shown in ruins. Ahab and Jezebel, king and queen of northern Israel, encouraged idol worship among their subjects.

Ben Sirach Praises Isaiah

Ben Sirach was a great sage who lived about 200 B.C. He wrote or compiled an apocryphal book called Wisdom of Ben Sirach or Ecclesiasticus.

"[Isaiah was] . . . a great man trustworthy in his vision. . . . By the power of the spirit he saw the last things. He comforted the mourners in Zion, he revealed what was to occur to the end of time, and hidden things long before they happened" (Ecclesiasticus 48:22–25).

The Righteous Praise the Lord in Prayer

This beautiful prayer or hymn presents an example of how the Lord's disciples may praise and worship him. It sets forth God's attributes, including his exaltation, righteousness, strength, and salvation.

Isaiah 33:2–6

O Lord, be gracious unto us;
we have waited for thee:
be thou [our] arm every morning,
our salvation also in the time of trouble. . . .
The Lord is exalted; for he dwelleth on high:
he hath filled Zion with judgment and righteousness.
And wisdom and knowledge shall be the stability of thy times,
    and strength of salvation:
the fear of the Lord is his treasure.

ISAIAH 33:4

And your spoil shall be gathered like the gathering of the caterpillar.

Isaiah 33:2–6 is a wonderful prayer from the righteous to the Lord. Its words exemplify how Saints may praise and worship the Lord. It sets forth the attributes of God, including his graciousness, strength, salvation, exaltation, justice, and righteousness. The prayer begins with the words: "O Lord, be gracious unto us; we have waited for thee: be thou their arm every morning, our salvation also in the time of trouble" (v. 2).

Verse 4 of the prayer has an interesting image of a caterpillar gathering sustenance for itself: "And your spoil shall be like the gathering of the caterpillar." "Spoil" generally refers to goods taken from an enemy during war. In this context it may refer to spiritual benefits, including peace, joy, and love, that the righteous receive as they partake of the Lord's salvation. The righteous, then, pray that they will receive this spiritual spoil just as the caterpillar gathers sustenance.

Left: Caterpillars on the Mount of Beatitudes. Caterpillars are wormlike larvae that can develop into locusts or grasshoppers. These creatures have been known to devour entire crops, and they sometimes represent God's judgments on the wicked.

ISAIAH 40:3

The voice of him that crieth in the wilderness, Prepare ye the way of the Lord, make straight in the desert a highway for our God.

The "voice of him that crieth in the wilderness" is that of John the Baptist, who during his mortal ministry cried repentance to the people (John 1:6–24; Mark 1:1–8; Luke 1:76–79). The "voice" also pertains to others besides John (D&C 33:10; 88:66).

The statement "prepare ye the way of the Lord" is a commission to prepare for the coming of the Lord by crying repentance and gathering a people sufficiently prepared by covenant and ordinance to receive him (Malachi 3:1; Luke 3:4–10 JST; D&C 84:28). John the Baptist prepared the way for the Lord's first coming. John also prepared the way of the Lord when he appeared to Joseph Smith to restore the keys of the Aaronic Priesthood. This commenced the preparation for the Lord's second coming (D&C 13).

The phrase "make straight in the desert a highway for our God" also means "prepare the way of the Lord." The people of the last days are to prepare for the second coming by making the path back to God's presence level or smooth. In other words, they are to remove obstacles so that others can be obedient to the laws and ordinances of the gospel.

Joseph Smith Speaks of Isaiah

"We believe the old prophet [Isaiah] verily told the truth."

Source: *Joseph Smith's Commentary on the Bible,* 51.

Below: Wilderness of Judea, near the northwest shore of the Dead Sea. The wilderness of Judea covers an area approximately thirty miles long by ten miles wide. The Negev desert surrounds it on the south, the hill country of Ephraim on the north, the Dead Sea on the east, and the hill country of Judah on the west. This wilderness receives very little rainfall, providing meager forage for flocks and very little water for Bedouin who still pitch their tents there. John the Baptist probably taught the gospel in this wilderness, and Jesus fasted here for forty days.

Above: An eagle flies above the mountain tops.

Above: Eagle, Hai-Bar Yotvata Nature Reserve. Four varieties of eagles live in the Holy Land today. The eagle's wing-span, up to seven and a half feet, enables the bird to travel great distances with much speed. Eagles are known for the protection and care they provide to their young.

ISAIAH 40:31

But they that wait upon the Lord shall renew their strength; they shall mount up with wings as eagles; they shall run, and not be weary; and they shall walk, and not faint.

These four beautiful promises, "renew," "mount up," "run," and "walk," are directed to those who "wait upon the Lord," or seek righteousness. The promises certainly pertain to the physical body (D&C 89:20). They also deal with the mind and spirit, which are continually renewed as his servants seek the Lord through righteous living and obedience to his commandments. The Lord's servants are compared to the eagle—they will be spiritually powerful and sustained.

I will plant in the wilderness the cedar, the shittah tree, and the myrtle, and the oil tree; I will set in the desert the fir tree, and the pine, and the box tree together: That they may see, and know, and consider, and understand together, that the hand of the Lord hath done this, and the Holy One of Israel hath created it.

The seven trees Isaiah lists represent righteous people. (See Psalm 1:1–3 for another instance of trees representing people.) Seven is a symbolic number that denotes wholeness or completion. These trees "see," "know," "consider," and "understand" together. Note the Lord's interest in the trees and his active role with them. He "will plant" and "will set" the trees in the wilderness so that all will know "the hand of the Lord hath done this, and the Holy One of Israel hath created it."

Below: An acacia tree in the Rift Valley, south of the Dead Sea. The acacia is a valuable hardwood that was used for building various parts of the tabernacle used by Moses and the children of Israel. The ark of the covenant, made of acacia wood, stood in the tabernacle's holy of holies. The table of shewbread that held twelve loaves of bread, and the altar of incense, also made of acacia, were located in the holy place. All three furnishings—the ark, table, and altar—were overlaid with pure gold (Exodus 25:1–30; 1–5).

Below: The forests of Carmel. Fir trees mentioned in the King James Version of the Bible seem to refer generally to coniferous trees. Fir trees provided fuel for cooking and heating as well as lumber for building. Solomon's builders, for example, used the lumber of fir trees to construct the two doors of the temple (1 Kings 6:34).

ISAIAH 48:18

O that thou hadst hearkened to my commandments! then had thy peace been as a river, and thy righteousness as the waves of the sea.

Peace of conscience and spirit are gifts God gives to those who are obedient (Isaiah 26:3; Psalm 37:37; Romans 8:6; 14:17–19; Philippians 4:7). That kind of peace comes from the Holy Spirit and is made available through the power of Christ and his atonement (John 14:27; 16:33). God's peace is not offered for this world alone. The peace spoken of here continues into celestial glory and will be consistent, ever flowing, like a river (Isaiah 66:12).

When people obey the Lord's commandments their righteousness is as unstoppable as the ocean waves. Also, their righteousness is truly subject to the pull of the heavens, as the waves are subject to the moon.

ISAIAH 49:10

They shall not hunger nor thirst; neither shall the heat nor sun smite them: for he that hath mercy on them shall lead them, even by the springs of water shall he guide them.

This passage refers to the Lord's blessings for those who are returning from exile, as well as for those returning from spiritual bondage. In physical captivity, exiles suffer from hunger and thirst. The heat of the sun threatens them. Spiritual exiles thirst for gospel truth and peace. The Lord protects and nourishes them. In all circumstances, it is only through Christ that spiritual hunger can be satisfied (John 6:35; Alma 31:38; 32:42; 3 Nephi 12:6; 20:8). The expression "springs of water" symbolizes living water (Isaiah 35:6–7; 41:17–18; 43:19–20), or Jesus Christ.

Left: A view of the Mediterranean Sea coast, near ancient Joppa. Both Isaiah and Lehi liken bodies of water to persons. Lehi says to Laman, "O that thou mightest be like unto this river, continually running into the fountain of all righteousness!" (1 Nephi 2:9). Isaiah writes: "O that thou hadst hearkened to my commandments! then had thy peace been as a river" (Isaiah 48:18).

Nephi's Keys to Understanding Isaiah

2 Nephi 25:1–8

1) Know the "manner of prophesying among the Jews" (v. 1).
2) Do not do "works of darkness" or "doings of abominations" (v. 2).
3) Be filled with the "spirit of prophecy" (v. 4).
4) Be familiar with the regions around Jerusalem (v. 6).
5) Live during the days that the prophecies of Isaiah are fulfilled (v. 7).

Below: The Jordan River, just south of the Sea of Galilee. The Jordan River was an important water system in the Holy Land that still serves the needs of communities in the region.

Personal Names

Abraham	29:22; 41:8
Adrammelech	37:38
Ahaz	1:1; 7:12
Ammon	11:14
Amoz	1:1; 2:1
Asaph	36:22
Baladan	39:1
Cyrus	44:28; 45:1
David	7:2, 13
Eliakim	22:20; 36:3
Ephraim	9:21
Esar-haddon	37:38
Hezekiah	1:1; 36:1
Hilkiah	22:20; 36:3
Immanuel	7:14; 8:8
Isaiah	1:1; 28:3
Jacob	2:3, 5
Jeberechiah	8:2
Jesse	11:10
Joah	36:3, 11
Jotham	1:1; 7:1
Lucifer	14:12
Maher-shalal-hash-baz	8:1
Manasseh	9:21
Merodach-baladan	39:1
Moses	63:11–12
Naphtali	9:1
Noah	54:9
Pekah	7:1
Rabshakeh	36:2, 4
Remaliah	7:1, 4
Rezin	7:1, 4
Sarah	51:2
Sargon	20:1
Saul	10:29
Sennacherib	36:1; 37:17
Sharezer	37:38
Shear-jashub	7:3
Shebna	22:15–16
Tabeal	7:6
Tartan	20:1
Tirhakah	37:9
Uriah	8:2
Uzziah	1:1; 6:1
Zechariah	8:2

Above: Assyrian palace relief, Nineveh. The relief portrays Assyrian soldiers using slings against inhabitants of the kingdom of Judah during Isaiah's ministry. Some Assyrian soldiers specialized in hurling stones with a sling, an accurate and deadly weapon with an endless supply of ammunition.

ISAIAH 51:1−2

Hearken to me, ye that follow after righteousness, ye that seek the Lord: look unto the rock whence ye are hewn, and to the hole of the pit whence ye are digged. Look unto Abraham your father, and unto Sarah that bare you: for I called him alone, and blessed him, and increased him.

Isaiah 51 is a call to those who "follow after righteousness." The call is repeated again and again: "hearken," "look," "hearken," "lift up your eyes," and again "hearken" (vv. 1–7). The call reminds the righteous that they are descendants of Abraham and Sarah and heirs to the blessings of the Abrahamic covenant. Their rock and quarry are Abraham and Sarah, from whom they descend. Even as Abraham and Sarah received promises when fulfillment seemed beyond hope, so will the Lord fulfill his promises to comfort Zion (v. 3).

Ultimately, of course, the rock from which the righteous come is God the Father, and Christ, who is called the Rock at least thirty-four times in the scriptures. For example, the Lord informed Enoch, "I am Messiah, the King of Zion, the Rock of Heaven, which is broad as eternity" (Moses 7:53).

ISAIAH 54:17

No weapon that is formed against thee shall prosper; and every tongue that shall rise against thee in judgment thou shalt condemn. This is the heritage of the servants of the Lord, and their righteousness is of me, saith the Lord.

The Lord speaks to the righteous and promises them protection from any weapon that is formed against them. This promise was repeated to Joseph Smith and Sidney Rigdon. The Lord said, "Verily, thus saith the Lord unto you—there is no weapon that is formed against you shall prosper" (D&C 71:9).

And Joseph Smith prayed on behalf of those who would worship in the temple, "We ask thee, Holy Father, to establish the people that shall worship, and honorably hold a name and standing in this thy house . . . that no weapon formed against them shall prosper" (D&C 109:24–25). Weapons, of course, take many forms, including instruments of physical harm and destruction or unseen powers of darkness.

Above: An ancient quarry, near the traditional tomb of Samuel the Prophet. Quarries from Old Testament times have been located at Megiddo, Samaria, Jerusalem, Nabi Samuel, and other places. Stonemasons made deep vertical cuts on the four sides of a premeasured block of stone and then separated the bottom part of the stone with wedges. The stone was then hauled to the construction site, where it was carefully shaped.

Armor and Defense

armour	22:8; 39:2
arrow(s)	5:2; 7:24
bow(s)	5:28; 7:24
breastplate	59:17
fort(s)	29:3; 32:14
gate(s)	14:31; 22:7
helmet	59:17
munition(s)	29:7; 33:16
quiver	22:6; 49:2
rod	9:4; 10:5
shaft	49:2
shield(s)	21:5; 22:6
sword	1:20; 2:4
wall(s)	2:15; 5:5
weapon(s)	13:5; 54:17

Clothing Terms

apparel	3:22; 4:1
bag	46:6
bracelets	3:19
bonnets	3:20
cauls	3:18
chains	3:19
clokes	59:17
clothe(s)	22:21; 49:18
crisping pins	3:22
crown	28:1
diadem	28:5
durable clothing	23:18
earrings	3:20
headbands	3:20
hoods	3:23
garment(s)	50:9; 51:6
girdle	3:24; 5:27
jewels	3:21; 61:10
mantles	3:22
mufflers	3:19
ointment	1:6; 39:2
ornaments	3:18
nose jewels	3:21
raiment	14:19; 63:3
rings	3:21
robe	22:21; 61:10
sackcloth	3:24; 15:3
shoe	20:2
shoe latchet	5:27
stomacher	3:24
train	6:1
vails	3:23
wimples	3:22

Musical Terms

harp	5:12; 24:8
instruments	38:20
pipe	5:12; 30:29
sing	5:1; 12:5
song	5:1; 12:2
tabret	5:12; 24:8
trumpet(s)	18:3; 27:13
viols	5:12; 14:11

ISAIAH 58:5

Is it such a fast that I have chosen? a day for a man to afflict his soul? is it to bow down his head as a bulrush, and to spread sackcloth and ashes under him? wilt thou call this a fast, and an acceptable day to the Lord?

Chapter 58 of Isaiah outlines the true law of the fast. Fasting involves far more than simply abstaining from two meals. Participants in a true fast seek to help and bless others. They remove heavy burdens from the shoulders of others. They share their substance. If they do these things, they will be blessed spiritually and temporally. Their portion of light will increase. Their health will be strengthened and the Lord will be their guide in all things.

Verse 5 indicates that they are not to put on an appearance of one who is making a sacrifice. True fasting does not consist of outward signs such as hanging one's head like a bent bulrush to give the appearance of suffering and to attract the attention of others.

Above: Bent bulrushes near the northwest shore of the Dead Sea. Reeds and bulrushes are hollow-stemmed grasses in swamplands or along the banks of rivers or ponds. They sometimes grow to a height of twenty feet. The ancients used reeds and bulrushes to create fishing poles, quills or pens, mats, musical instruments, and baskets.

ISAIAH 58:6–7

Is not this the fast that I have chosen? . . . Is it not to deal thy bread to the hungry, and that thou bring the poor that are cast out to thy house? when thou seest the naked, that thou cover him; and that thou hide not thyself from thine own flesh?

Above: A Bedouin woman and her children beg for food, Sinai desert. Unfortunately, many have to beg to eat.

This verse details four actions of a true fast before the Lord: (1) giving bread to the hungry, where bread represents food generally; (2) assisting the poor; (3) covering the naked, meaning providing the destitute with clothing through fast offerings; and (4) helping family members in need, or in Isaiah's words, "[hiding] not thyself from thine own flesh." These four actions are the essence of pure religion (Matthew 25:31–46; James 1:27). Those who have done these things will receive God's blessings. Isaiah lists some of those blessings. For example, their fasting will be recognized and their prayers heard (Isaiah 58:8–12; see also Ezekiel 18:5–9, 16–17).

Above: Flat bread, Old City, Jerusalem. Bread was a staple food for ancient Israelites. Barley was the most common grain used in bread, although wheat was also prevalent. Fresh produce was not as available as it is today, although grapes, figs, cucumbers, and olives were abundant.

Above: Waters flow through Tel Dan. Perennial springs are uncommon in the Holy Land. They are so important to the stability and well-being of a community that some cities, including Jericho, Megiddo, Gezer, and Jerusalem, were built around them. A story from 2 Kings 2:19–22 illustrates the significance of a spring of water to a particular settlement. For a period of time Jericho's perennial spring produced toxic waters that brought "death" and "barren land." The prophet Elisha, a visitor to Jericho, heard about this spring, so he cast salt into the water, uttering these words: "Thus saith the Lord, I have healed these waters; there shall not be from thence any more death or barren land."

Below: Section of garden at the Garden Tomb, Jerusalem.

ISAIAH 58:11

And the Lord shall guide thee continually, and satisfy thy soul in drought, and make fat thy bones: and thou shalt be like a watered garden, and like a spring of water, whose waters fail not.

This verse describes four blessings to those who live the true law of the fast before the Lord: the Lord will guide them, he will satisfy their souls in drought, he will make fat their bones, and he will make them like a watered garden or spring of water. The Lord provides living water in times of spiritual drought. Bones were considered the gauge of the body's vitality—they become dry and brittle with age and illness but are moist and supple with youth, health, and vigor (Job 21:24). Bones that are made fat are renewed and made strong (Isaiah 66:14). "Make fat thy bones" may also refer to the resurrection, when dead bones will be renewed with life.

Isaiah says the righteous will be like a "watered garden" and a "spring." In a garden, water, the source of life, often comes from the outside. It is the same for the righteous, who receive sustenance from the Lord (Isaiah 51:3; Numbers 24:5–6). Jesus said, "He that believeth on me, as the scripture hath said, out of his belly shall flow rivers of living water" (John 7:38). In this dispensation the Lord promised, "Unto him that keepeth my commandments I will give the mysteries of my kingdom, and the same shall be in him a well of living water, springing up unto everlasting life" (D&C 63:23).

ISAIAH 65:8

Thus saith the Lord, As the new wine is found in the cluster, and one saith, Destroy it not; for a blessing is in it: so will I do for my servants' sakes, that I may not destroy them all.

Israel is the Lord's vineyard (Isaiah 5:1; 27:2), which has produced mostly wild grapes useless for wine. But there have always been a few who remain faithful to the Lord and his law. For the sake of these few good grapes, the Lord has refrained from altogether destroying the vineyard. In the end, though, only the good clusters will be saved, and the rest will be destroyed (Isaiah 1:9, 27–28; 4:3–4).

The expression "destroy it not; for a blessing is in it," may have been part of a vintage song. (Isaiah 16:10 and Jeremiah 25:30 suggest that those who worked in vineyards sang and shouted.) The grape cluster should not be destroyed because of the good juice in it. This image symbolizes the Lord's treatment of Israel—he promises not to destroy the whole of Israel because of the good people who remain.

ISAIAH 65:10

And Sharon shall be a fold of flocks, and the valley of Achor a place for the herds to lie down in, for my people that have sought me.

Isaiah 65:8–10 is a prophecy about God's covenant people. He refers to them as "my servants," "Jacob," "Judah," "an inheritor," "mine elect," and "my people." The Lord promises to provide an inheritance for his elect (v. 9) and a safe place for the righteous.

Sharon is the coastal plain from Carmel south to Joppa. The Israelites marched through the valley of Achor (perhaps Wadi Qelt), on the east, to get from Jericho to Jerusalem (Joshua 7:24; 15:7). Isaiah expresses, then, that the whole land from east to west, will become a place of safety and refuge for the Lord's people. It will become like a gigantic sheepfold for those who seek the Lord. They will find pasture, water, and safety there, because Jesus Christ himself will be their Shepherd.

Above: Cluster of grapes, near Hebron. Because of his multiple references to vineyards, vines, and vinedressers, it is apparent that Isaiah is very familiar with grape cultivation. In Isaiah 5:1–7, for example, he describes the preparation of a fertile hill for the planting of a vineyard.

Right: A sheepfold, northeast of Lachish. This fold consists of a man-made stone fence (now broken down, foreground) and a three-sided sheer wall. Jesus spoke of a sheepfold in one of his parables; he himself is the door of the sheepfold (John 10:1–10).

THE EARTHLY MINISTRY OF JESUS CHRIST

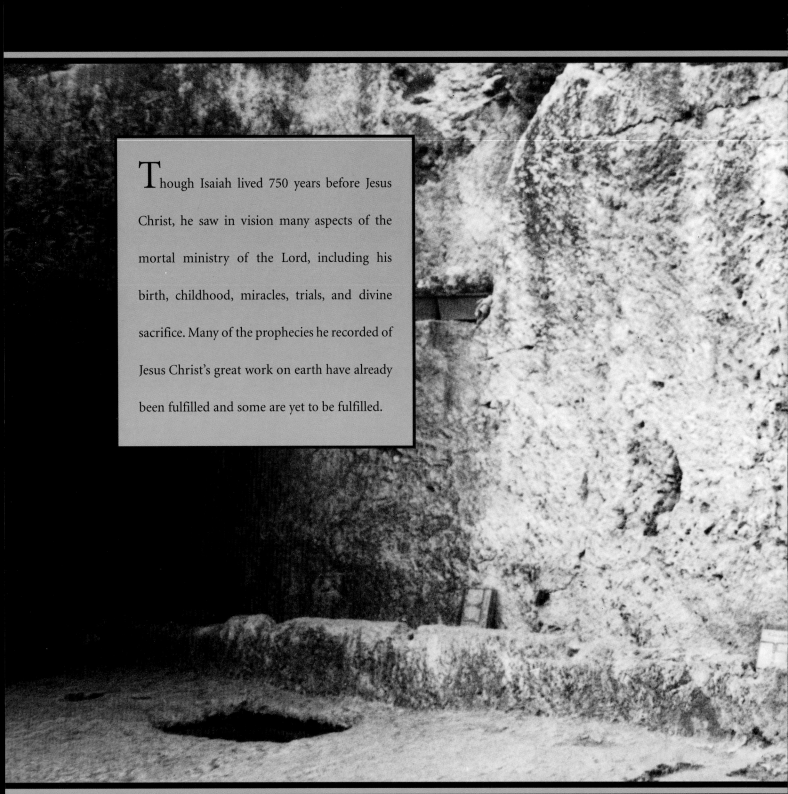

Though Isaiah lived 750 years before Jesus Christ, he saw in vision many aspects of the mortal ministry of the Lord, including his birth, childhood, miracles, trials, and divine sacrifice. Many of the prophecies he recorded of Jesus Christ's great work on earth have already been fulfilled and some are yet to be fulfilled.

Garden Tomb, east Jerusalem.

Above: Lambs in Jerusalem. Lamb's wool, when groomed and washed, becomes snow-white.

Come now, and let us reason together, saith the Lord: though your sins be as scarlet, they shall be as white as snow; though they be red like crimson, they shall be as wool.

In this passage scarlet, a bright red, and crimson, a deep red, are both used to symbolize blood, which in turn can signify sin. The sins of the children of Israel were both conspicuous and deep-seated. The Lord, through Isaiah, contrasts the bloodlike reds of scarlet and crimson with pure white snow and wool.

White symbolizes purity, innocence, and light. In addition, wool, a product from a lamb, points to the atonement of Jesus, the "Lamb of God, which taketh away the sin of the world" (John 1:29). The contrast between red and white illustrates the power of Christ's atonement to make the penitent sinner clean.

Above: The dyeing process does not work properly with gray, black, or tan wool. Only white wool will ensure the dyed wool takes on the desired color. The wool was soaked in vats of dye and then hung up to dry. In ancient times, the crimson and scarlet dyes were made from worms or grubs that fed on and covered the branches of oak trees.

ISAIAH 8:14

And he shall be for a sanctuary; but for a stone of stumbling and for a rock of offence to both the houses of Israel.

To the righteous, Jesus Christ is the elect and precious chief cornerstone "upon which they might build and have safe foundation" (Jacob 4:15). But to those who reject his word, Jesus is "a stone of stumbling, and a rock of offence" (1 Peter 2:6–8; 1 Corinthians 1:23).

The phrase "both the houses of Israel" refers to the northern kingdom of Israel and the southern kingdom of Judah. During times of apostasy, citizens of these kingdoms viewed Jesus Christ as a stumbling stone, or someone who got in their way during their journey through mortality.

Above: This well-worn path near Montfort, northern Israel, is filled with stumbling stones that may cause path users to trip and fall. Stumbling stones were much more common for travelers in the ancient world than now, with today's numerous cement sidewalks and paved roads.

Sources of Symbolism for Isaiah

Symbolism is a key element of Isaiah's text. It appears to be part of every single revelation. Through revelation, Isaiah drew upon his social, cultural, religious, and political background to produce hundreds of different symbols. He used items that deal with common aspects of life to illustrate prophecy and eternal truths. The kinds of symbols Isaiah used seem to come from all areas of life. Following are twenty-three categories of Isaiah's symbols, with a few examples in each.

Common actions: drinking, eating, falling down, fornicating, shaving hair, singing, sitting

Sacred actions: anointing, ordaining, sacrificing, spreading forth hands

Animals: asses, bear, beast, bee, bird, bittern, bullock, calf, camels, cattle, crane

Architectural elements: bulwarks, foundation, gate, house, pillar, wall, watchtower, windows

Armor and weaponry: armor, arrow, bow, shield, sword, weapon

Astronomical elements: cloud, constellations, heaven, moon, stars, sun

Atmospheric or geologic conditions: earthquake, flood, hail, storm, tempest, whirlwinds, wind

Colors: crimson, red, scarlet, white

Ecclesiastical offices: priests, prophet

Elements/rocks/minerals: ashes, clay, clods, dirt, gold, iron, rock, silver, tin

Family and social relationships: bridegroom, brother, children, daughter, father, firstborn, handmaids

Foods: barley, berries, bread, butter, corn, fruit, grapes, honey, milk, wheat, wine

Topography: brook, cities, deep, desert, dry ground, field, highways, hill, mountain, river

Human anatomy: arm, beard, belly, blood, bones, cheeks, ear, eye, face, feet, finger, heart

Names and titles of deity: Immanuel, Jehovah, Wonderful

Names and titles of persons: Beulah, Cyrus, Lucifer, Abraham, Cyrus, David, Jesse, Sarah

Numbers: thousand, hundred

Common objects: ax, bed, bill of divorcement, book, chains, chariots, cup, idol

Sacred objects: altar, drink offering, incense, temple

Occupations: carpenter, creditors, fishermen, harvester, king, officers, seller, servant

Places: Ariel, Assyria, Babylon, Egypt, Jerusalem, Sodom, Tarshish

Plants: cedars, fig tree, flower, grass, groves, leaf, oak, olive tree, orchard, root, seed

Time: day, daytime, night, noonday, summer, winter

Source: Adapted from Donald W. Parry, Jay A. Parry, and Tina M. Peterson, *Understanding Isaiah*, 604–6.

Above: Three men winnowing wheat, part of the harvesting process, near Jericho. Note the joy on the face of the man on the left. After grain is harvested, it is threshed, loosening or separating the seeds' chaff, or husks. After the threshing, the grain is winnowed, a process that removes the chaff from the grain.

One common method of winnowing in ancient times consisted of placing the threshed grain in a mound and then tossing it into the air during a breezy day. The wind carried the lighter chaff away while the heavier kernels of grain fell back to the ground, where they were gathered into jars or granaries. The entire process of harvesting caused much joy among the people, as it ensured them food for the coming year.

ISAIAH 9:1–2

The people that walked in darkness have seen a great light: they that dwell in the land of the shadow of death, upon them hath the light shined.

The land of the shadow of death is a land peopled by those who do not know Jesus Christ, the "great light," and his gospel. These people walk in darkness. Jesus was the great light that shone upon the inhabitants of Galilee during his mortal mission. Matthew 4:13–16 contains the fulfillment of this prophecy found in Isaiah 9:1–2. As those who follow Christ walk through mortality in the latter days, they will receive great hope, comfort, and joy when they accept Jesus as the "great light."

Left: The sun rises over the mountains of Moab, illuminating the Dead Sea.

ISAIAH 9:3

Thou hast multiplied the nation, and not increased the joy: they joy before thee according to the joy in harvest.

Isaiah 9 presents a joyous messianic prophecy. The familiar words "for unto us a child is born, unto us a son is given" (v. 6) are part of this prophecy and foretell the coming of the Savior. Because of Jesus Christ's coming, joy will increase (v. 3). The Messiah will break the rod of the oppressor (v. 4). The soldiers' boots, garments, and other items of war will be burned with fire (v. 5). A child who will establish his righteous government and peace among the nations will be born (vv. 6–7; Luke 2:10–11). The Prince of Peace will reign.

The Lord's victory over Israel's enemies and his coming will bring Israel a joy similar to that experienced by a farmer at an abundant harvest.

ISAIAH 9:4

For thou hast broken the yoke of his burden, and the staff of his shoulder, the rod of his oppressor, as in the day of Midian.

In biblical times, the staff and rod were used by taskmasters on slaves. A yoke was a wooden frame designed to harness together beasts of burden. These three items—the yoke, staff, and rod—signify oppression, or the burdens placed on Israel by its neighbors (Isaiah 10:5, 24–27).

In particular, the language of this verse recalls the manner in which Egypt oppressed the Israelites before Moses led them out of captivity. (For example, see "yoke" in Leviticus 26:13; "burden" in Exodus 1:11; 2:11; 5:4–5; 6:6–7; and "taskmasters" in Exodus 3:7; 5:6, 10–14). Just as Moses delivered ancient Israel from the Egyptian yoke of physical bondage, Jesus Christ delivers his followers from the yoke of spiritual bondage.

Government Terms

ambassadors	18:2; 30:4
government	9:7
judge(s)	1:17, 23
king(s)	1:1; 6:1
law	8:16
lawgiver	33:22
prince(s)	3:4; 9:6
queens	49:23
ruler(s)	1:10; 14:5
sceptre	14:5
scribe	33:18; 36:3

Above: Pair of yokes with crossbar and other attachments, Jericho. A yoke is a wooden frame designed to harness animals, such as oxen or asses, to wheeled vehicles, plows, or other agricultural implements.

Isaiah Mentions the Following Body Parts of the Lord

arm	30:30; 33:2; 40:10–11; 48:14; 51:9; 63:5	ears	37:17; 50:4	lips	11:4; 30:27
		eyes	37:17	mouth	1:20; 11:4; 40:5; 58:14
back	50:6	face	8:17; 50:6–7; 59:2; 64:7	soul	1:14
bosom	40:11	feet	60:13	tongue	30:27; 50:4
bowels	63:15	hair	50:6	voice	6:8; 30:31; 66:6
breath	30:33	hand	1:25; 5:25; 8:11; 9:12		
cheeks	50:6	head	59:17		

And there shall come forth a rod out of the stem of Jesse, and a Branch shall grow out of his roots.

The discussion of the tree, its rod, stem, branch, and roots in Isaiah 11:1 is a continuation of the prophecy regarding the cutting down of the forest from the previous chapter. The Lord will "lop the bough," hew down the "high ones," and "cut down the thickets of the forest" (Isaiah 10:33–34). The Lord, or forester, will trim the boughs and cut down the trees to clean out the forest and prepare the way for the stem of Jesse to flourish. This trimming and cutting symbolizes the Lord's severing the power and glory of unrighteous leaders and their nations.

The stem of Jesse is Christ. The Doctrine and Covenants is explicit: "Who is the Stem of Jesse spoken of in the 1st, 2d, 3d, 4th, and 5th verses of the 11th chapter of Isaiah? Verily thus saith the Lord: It is Christ" (D&C 113:1–2). The Davidic royal family, then, is compared to the stump or "stem" of an olive tree. Just as an olive tree is able to send forth a shoot or "rod," so would the family of David send forth a leader who would have wisdom, understanding, counsel, might, and knowledge (Isaiah 11:2). That leader is Jesus Christ.

Below and right: Old olive trees, Garden of Gethsemane, Jerusalem. Note the rods or branches growing out of the trunk of each tree. When the olive tree is cut down, new shoots grow out of both its old trunk as well as its far-reaching root system.

Olive trees grow to a height of about eighteen feet and live for centuries. The trees' thick, gnarled trunks produce numerous branches. Olivewood is a valuable source of lumber for artisans and craftsmen. For instance, artisans carved the cherubim that were housed in the holy of holies of Solomon's temple from olivewood. The cherubim were then overlaid with pure gold. Oil produced from olives was an important food source and was used in oil lamps. Ceremonially, olive oil was used for the coronation of kings and the ritual anointing of persons and things in ancient temples.

Therefore thus saith the Lord God, Behold, I lay in Zion for a foundation a stone, a tried stone, a precious corner stone, a sure foundation.

This is a prophecy about Jesus Christ, who is called a "stone," a "tried stone," and a "precious corner stone." A tried stone withstands a test of strength, and a cornerstone adds permanence and strength to the foundation of a building. Here the building is Zion, where "he that believeth" may have a "sure foundation" on which to build (1 Peter 2:6–8). Paul's imagery accords with that of Isaiah and Peter. Paul says that the church was built "upon the foundation of the apostles and prophets, Jesus Christ himself being the chief corner stone" (Ephesians 2:20).

Above: Foundation and cornerstones, Tel Dan, probably built at the time of King Jeroboam, ca. 953 B.C.

Above: Huge Herodian cornerstones (first century B.C.) at the southwest corner of the Temple Mount, Jerusalem. Structurally, the cornerstones and foundation represent the most important parts of any building. Without them sections of a building may tumble.

From the Book of Isaiah	Fulfilled and Recorded in New Testament Books
"Behold, a virgin shall conceive." (Isaiah 7:14)	"A virgin shall be with child." (Matthew 1:23)
"beyond Jordan, in Galilee of the nations" (Isaiah 9:1, 2)	"And leaving Nazareth, he came and dwelt in Capernaum . . . beyond Jordan, Galilee of the Gentiles." (Matthew 4:13, 15–16)
"Of the increase of his government and peace there shall be no end, upon the throne of David, and upon his kingdom." (Isaiah 9:7)	"And the Lord God shall give unto him the throne of his father David. And he shall reign . . . for ever; and of his kingdom there shall be no end." (Luke 1:32, 33)
"The voice of him that crieth in the wilderness" (Isaiah 40:3)	"He said, I am the voice of one crying in the wilderness." (John 1:23)
"I hid not my face from shame and spitting." (Isaiah 50:6)	"Then did they spit in his face, and buffeted him." (Matthew 26:67)
"Behold, my servant shall deal prudently, he shall be exalted." (Isaiah 52:13)	"Wherefore God also hath highly exalted him." (Philippians 2:9)
"Who hath believed our report? and to whom is the arm of the Lord revealed?" (Isaiah 53:1)	"That the saying of Esaias the prophet might be fulfilled, which he spake, Lord, who hath believed our report? and to whom hath the arm of the Lord been revealed?" (John 12:38)
"Surely he hath borne our griefs and carried our sorrows . . . and with his stripes we are healed." (Isaiah 53:4–5)	"His own self bare our sins in his own body on the tree, that we, being dead to sins, should live unto righteousness: by whose stripes ye were healed." (1 Peter 2:24)
"All we like sheep have gone astray." (Isaiah 53:6)	"For ye were as sheep going astray." (1 Peter 2:25)
"He was oppressed, and he was afflicted, yet he opened not his mouth: he is brought as a lamb to the slaughter, and as a sheep before her shearers is dumb, so he openeth not his mouth." (Isaiah 53:7)	"And Pilate asked him again, saying, Answerest thou nothing? behold how many things they witness against thee. But Jesus answered nothing; so that Pilate marveled." (Mark 15:4–5)
"And he made his grave with the wicked, and with the rich in his death." (Isaiah 53:9)	"When the even was come, there came a rich man of Arimathaea, named Joseph. . . . And when Joseph had taken the body, he wrapped it in a clean linen cloth, And laid it in his own new tomb, which he had hewn out in the rock." (Matthew 27:57, 59–60)
"and he was numbered with the transgressors" (Isaiah 53:12)	"And with him they crucify two thieves; the one on his right hand, and the other on his left. And the scripture was fulfilled, which saith, And he was numbered with the transgressors." (Mark 15:27–28)
"The Spirit of the Lord God is upon me; because the Lord hath anointed me to preach good tidings unto the meek." (Isaiah 61:1)	"And there was delivered unto him the book of the prophet Esaias. And when he had opened the book, he found the place where it was written, The Spirit of the Lord is upon me, because he hath anointed me to preach the gospel to the poor." (Luke 4:17–18)
"And he said, Go, and tell this people, Hear ye indeed, but understand not; and see ye indeed, but perceive not. Make the heart of this people fat." (Isaiah 6:9–10)	"And in them is fulfilled the prophecy of Esaias, which saith, By hearing ye shall hear, and shall not understand; and seeing ye shall see, and shall not perceive: For this people's heart is waxed gross." (Matthew 13:14–15)
"And he shall be for a sanctuary; but for a stone of stumbling and for a rock of offence to both the house of Israel, for a gin and for a snare to the inhabitants of Jerusalem. And many among them shall stumble, and fall, and be broken, and be snared, and be taken." (Isaiah 8:14–15)	"As it is written, Behold, I lay in Sion a stumblingstone and rock of offence: and whosoever believeth on him shall not be ashamed. . . . And a stone of stumbling, and a rock of offence, even to them which stumble at the word, being disobedient: whereunto also they were appointed." (Romans 9:33; 1 Peter 2:8)
"And in that day there shall be a root of Jesse, which shall stand for an ensign of the people; to it shall the Gentiles seek: and his rest shall be glorious." (Isaiah 11:10)	"And again, Esaias saith, There shall be a root of Jesse, and he that shall rise to reign over the Gentiles; in him shall the Gentiles trust." (Romans 15:12)
"And the key of the house of David will I lay upon his shoulder; so he shall open, and none shall shut; and he shall shut, and none shall open." (Isaiah 22:22)	"These things saith he that is holy, he that is true, he that hath the key of David, he that openeth, and no man shutteth; and shutteth, and no man openeth." (Revelations 3:7)
"He will swallow up death in victory." (Isaiah 25:8)	"And this mortal shall have put on immortality, then shall be brought to pass the saying that is written, Death is swallowed up in victory." (1 Corinthians 15:54)
"Behold, I lay in Zion for a foundation a stone, a tried stone, a precious corner stone, a sure foundation: he that believeth shall not make haste." (Isaiah 28:16)	"Wherefore also it is contained in the scripture, Behold, I lay in Sion a chief corner stone, elect, precious: and he that believeth on him shall not be confounded." (1 Peter 2:6)

ISAIAH 28:24

Doth the plowman plow all day to sow? Doth he open and break the clods of his ground?

Isaiah presents the Parable of the Farmer in Isaiah 28:23–29. The Lord is the plowman who, like the farmer, performs all his work in its proper order, with specific results in mind. Through a rhetorical question in verse 24, Isaiah explains that a plowman does not plow continuously—literally all day, every day. If he did, the growing season would be over before the seeds were ever planted. The farmer must undertake many tasks to ensure a successful harvest. Similarly, the Lord follows a precise pattern as he deals with his people. Everything occurs in its proper order with specific results in mind.

Above: An old wooden plow with a rusted plowshare, Neot Kedumim, a biblical landscape reserve.

Below: A plowman, prodding his animal with a goad, works the soil near the highway between Bet Guvrin National Park and Jerusalem. The design of plows known from antiquity is very similar to the ones used in areas of the present-day Near East. The handle and crossbar were made of wood, and the plowshare was made of metal. Oxen, asses, or other beasts pulled the plow, which was guided by a farmer.

ISAIAH 32:1–2

Behold, a king shall reign in righteousness . . .
And a man shall be as an hiding place from the
wind, and a covert from the tempest; as rivers of
water in a dry place, as the shadow of a great
rock in a weary land.

Jesus Christ is the "king" and the "man" mentioned in the passage above. Isaiah provides four metaphors to indicate the Lord's temporal and spiritual preservation of the Saints: "hiding place" (or shelter), "covert," "rivers of water," and "shadow of a great rock." These correspond with "wind," "tempest," "dry place," and "weary land"—words that pertain to this earthly existence with all of its tribulation and hardships. When the Lord's followers are thirsty, the Lord will provide rivers of water to quench their thirst, and when they require rest, he will provide shadow beside a great rock. In other words, when they need shelter from the tempests of life, Jesus will be their refuge.

ISAIAH 40:11

[The Lord God] shall feed his flock like a shep-
herd: he shall gather the lambs with his arm,
and carry them in his bosom, and shall gently
lead those that are with young.

This passage compares the Lord to a shepherd and his people to lambs. The same images have been used by many other prophets in describing humanity's relationship with God (Psalms 23; 28:9; Jeremiah 23:3). Isaiah says that the Lord will do four things for his people: (1) he will feed them as a shepherd feeds his flock; (2) he will gather them with his arm; (3) he will carry them in his bosom, or the fold of the shepherd's robe, a symbol of intimate, loving care; and (4) he will lead those that are with young. That is to say, he will provide his people with temporal as well as spiritual sustenance.

Above: A weary traveler may find refuge from the sun, wind, or rain within this thicket on a trail south of Banias.

Right: A shepherd carries a sheep, Bethany. For thousands of years the Holy Land has supported a pastoral culture, shepherds caring for their flocks. Then, as now, shepherds guide their sheep to food and water and gather them into a fold at night for protection.

Above: An oil lamp with a faltering flame, Qatzrin, an ancient village from the talmudic period (ca. A.D. 200–500). Earthenware lamps, with linen wicks made of flax and olive oil for fuel, provided light for homes. A faltering flame or "smoking flax" signaled that the oil was about to run out.

Jesus Reads Isaiah in the Synagogue

This passage refers to Christ's mission to the weak.

Luke 4:16–21

"And [Jesus] came to Nazareth, where he had been brought up: and, as his custom was, he went into the synagogue on the sabbath day, and stood up for to read. And there was delivered unto him the book of the prophet Esaias [Isaiah]. And when he had opened the book, he found the place where it was written, The Spirit of the Lord God is upon me, because the Lord hath anointed me to preach the gospel to the poor; he hath sent me to heal the brokenhearted, to preach deliverance to the captives, and recovering of sight to the blind, to set at liberty them that are bruised, to preach the acceptable year of the Lord. And he closed the book . . . And he began to say unto them, This day is this scripture fulfilled in your ears."

ISAIAH 42:3

A bruised reed shall [the Lord] not break, and the smoking flax shall he not quench.

Isaiah had a great understanding of the Savior and his mission to strengthen those who were faltering. He knew that Jesus' mission would include serving the house of Israel and the gentiles. He knew that Christ would not fail his mission (Isaiah 42:1–9).

Isaiah introduces two images in Isaiah 42:3—a "bruised reed" and a "smoking flax." A reed is a marsh plant with tall, hollow stems. A bruised reed is one that is bent and cracked, and therefore weak. A bruised reed may represent physical weaknesses or afflictions. A smoking flax is a wick made from linen for an oil lamp, whose flame wavers, about to go out. This may signify someone who is spiritually weak, whose faith falters.

Jesus healed and cared for the physically infirm, and he taught and guided the spiritually weak. A reed requires much water to grow properly. A linen wick burns brightly when it has sufficient oil. Symbolically, Jesus Christ, as the water of life, provides water to the reed and, as the Anointed One, provides oil to the wick.

ISAIAH 44:22

I have blotted out, as a thick cloud, thy transgressions, and, as a cloud, thy sins: return unto me; for I have redeemed thee.

Isaiah 44:21–23 declares that the Lord has redeemed the house of Israel. In these verses the Lord reminds the children of Israel of their preferred status as his servants, adding that he will forgive them and forget their sins if they will return to him. The atonement has already been firmly decreed, and mankind's sins can be blotted out by the Redeemer. Because of this great gift of redemption, all God's creations sing praises to him (v. 23).

In verse 22, the Lord uses a universal image—a thick cloud—to illustrate how he is able to blot out sins. As a thick cloud blots out the sky, the Lord will blot out sins and remove them from his memory. A scripture revealed through Joseph Smith presents a similar message: "Behold, he who has repented of his sins, the same is forgiven, and I, the Lord, remember them no more" (D&C 58:42).

ISAIAH 53:2

For he shall grow up before him as a tender plant, and as a root out of a dry ground.

Isaiah 53 is one of the most detailed prophecies of the Messiah found in the Old Testament. It gives Isaiah's readers vast insight into the work of the mortal Jesus and the blessings he offers. Worshipers learn from this chapter that Jesus Christ would bear the transgressions and iniquities of all mankind. He would take the sins of his followers upon himself so that they could be cleansed. He would also bear their grief and sorrow, their emotional pain and suffering. If they would turn to him, he would heal them of all these infirmities.

Isaiah uses two plant metaphors to portray the young mortal Jesus: "tender plant" and "root." Jesus was like a tender plant, untouched by corruption and sin. He was subject to temptation, hunger, fatigue, sickness, and pain. The Father, however, watched over the young Jesus as a careful gardener watches a tender plant. Luke records: "The child grew, and waxed strong in spirit, filled with wisdom: and the grace of God was upon him" (Luke 2:40).

Jesus came forth not in fertile land, but in "dry ground," both temporally and spiritually. He grew up in the harsh conditions of an arid land and a spiritually barren nation. Dry ground is the opposite of streams of water, which usually denote temporal happiness and prosperity. Streams of water also represent the spiritual life brought by the gospel. The dry ground represents the spiritual barrenness of apostate Judaism.

Above: Tender plant at Wadi Qelt, the Judean desert.

The Many Names, Titles, and Symbols of Christ

Isaiah provides numerous names, titles, and symbols of Jesus Christ in his writings, many of them more than once. The names Holy One of Israel, God, Lord, Lord God, Lord of hosts, and Redeemer, for instance, each appear a dozen or more times in the book of Isaiah. Truly, Isaiah's writings are centered in Christ. Following is a representative list of names, titles, and symbols of Christ together with a reference from Isaiah.

Advocate (3:13)
Almighty (13:6)
Beloved (5:1)
Branch (11:1)
Bread (33:16)
Child (9:6)
Covert (32:2)
Creator (40:28)
Cyrus (45:1)
Elect (42:1)
Everlasting Father (9:6)
Everlasting God (40:28)
Everlasting light (60:19)
First (41:4)
First and Last (48:12)
Gin (8:14)
God (54:5)
God of Israel (37:16)
God of Jacob (2:3)
God of judgment (30:18)
God of the whole earth (54:5)
God of thy salvation (17:10)
God of truth (65:16)
God the Lord (42:5)
Great light (9:2)
Hiding place (32:2)
Holy One (12:6)
Holy One of Israel (1:4)
Holy One of Jacob (29:23)
Husband (54:5)
Immanuel (7:14)
Jehovah (12:2)
Judge (33:22)
King (6:5)
King of Israel (44:6)
King of Jacob (41:21)
Lamb (53:7)
Lawgiver (33:22)
Light (42:6)
Light of Israel (10:17)
Light to the Gentiles (49:6)
Lord (66:9)
Lord God (30:15)
Lord God of hosts (22:5)
Lord God of Israel (37:21)
Lord Jehovah (26:4)
Lord of hosts (22:25)

Lord the Creator (40:28)
Lord, the God of David (38:5)
Maher-shalal-hash-baz (8:1, 3)
Maker (54:5)
Mighty God (9:6)
Mighty One of Israel (1:24)
Mighty One of Jacob (49:26)
Man (32:2)
Man of sorrows (53:3)
Master (1:3)
Messenger (42:19)
Mighty God (9:6)
Most High (14:14)
Owner (1:3)
Prince of Peace (9:6)
Redeemer (41:14)
Redeemer of Israel (49:7)
Refuge (25:4)
Righteous man (41:2)
Righteous servant (53:11)
Rivers (43:19)
Rivers of water (32:2)
Rock of offence (8:14)
Rock of thy strength (17:10)
Root (53:2)
Salvation (12:2)
Sanctuary (8:14)
Saviour (43:3)
Servant (42:1)
Shadow (25:4)
Shepherd (40:11)
Snare (8:14)
Son (9:6)
Song (12:2)
Springs of water (49:10)
Stem of Jesse (11:1)
Stone (28:16)
Stone of stumbling (8:14)
Strength (12:2)
Sure foundation (28:16)
Teach[er] (48:17)
Tender plant (53:2)
Water (44:3)
Waters (8:6)
Well beloved (5:1)
Wells of salvation (12:3)
Wonderful Counselor (9:6)

Source: Donald W. Parry, Jay A. Parry, and Tina M. Peterson, *Understanding Isaiah*, 595–96.

Suffering of the Messiah

Isaiah 53 is one of the greatest prophecies of the Messiah found in scripture. It provides insight into the work of the mortal Messiah and the blessings he offers humanity. It states that the Messiah bore humanity's sickness, pains, and transgressions.

Isaiah 53:4–7

Surely he has borne our sicknesses,
and carried our pains;

but we esteemed him plagued,
smitten by God, and afflicted.

But he was pierced for our transgressions,
he was crushed for our iniquities.

The chastisement upon him made us whole,
and with his stripes we are healed.

All we like sheep have gone astray;
we have turned, each of us, to his own way; and
the Lord has laid on him the iniquities of
   us all.

He was oppressed,
and he was afflicted,

yet he opened not his mouth. He is led as a
   lamb to the slaughter,
and as a ewe before her shearers is dumb, yet
   he opened not his mouth.

Translation by Donald W. Parry

ISAIAH 53:5

But he was wounded for our transgressions.

Isaiah 53 comprises a detailed prophecy of the ministry, atoning sacrifice, and triumph of Jesus Christ. Verse 5 speaks concerning Christ's atoning sacrifice. The expression "he was wounded for our transgressions" may better be translated from the Hebrew as "he was pierced for our transgressions." Jesus Christ was pierced for the transgressions of all mankind while on the cross. The Psalmist prophesied: "They pierced my hands and my feet" (Psalm 22:16). In April 1829, Joseph Smith received this revelation from the Lord: "Behold the wounds which pierced my side, and also the prints of the nails in my hands and feet" (D&C 6:37).

Below: Isaiah prophesied that the Messiah would be wounded, or pierced, "for our transgressions," referring to Christ's crucifixion. This photo is of a "heel bone pierced by an iron nail, discovered in the tomb of a Jew named Yehohanan son of Hagkol . . . This intriguing find, dating back some 2,000 years, is the only archaeological evidence in the world for the practice of crucifixion" (*In the Path of Christianity*, Israel Museum [pamphlet, 2000]).

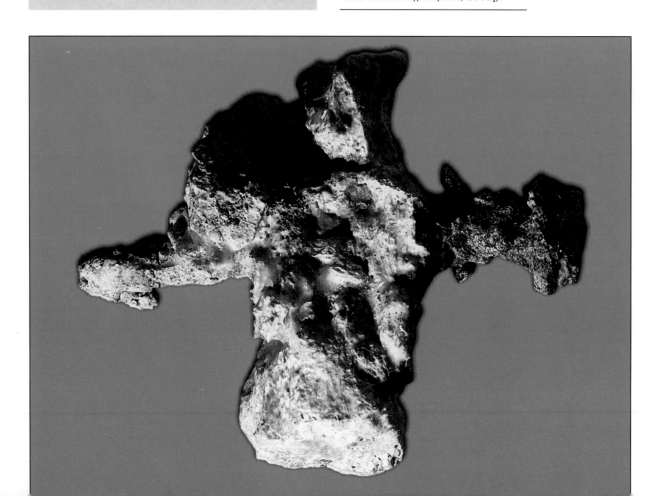

He was bruised for our iniquities.

The phrase "he was bruised for our iniquities" is more correctly rendered "he was crushed (Hebrew *daka*ʾ) for our iniquities." Jesus Christ was crushed in the Garden of Gethsemane. The word Gethsemane (Hebrew *Gath Shemen*) itself signifies "oil press." Just as olives are crushed at an olive press to render pure olive oil, so the Anointed One was crushed to sanctify mankind. He suffered so mightily in the Garden of Gethsemane that he bled from every pore (Luke 22:44; Mosiah 3:7; D&C 19:18).

Below: Olive press, Jerusalem Center for Near Eastern Studies. Olive oil runs into the stone basin near the top half of the press. Olive oil production consisted of two stages: crushing and pressing. Olives were first placed in a stone basin and then crushed by a huge stone wheel set on end that rolled over the olives. The crushed olives were removed from the stone basin and placed in baskets designed especially for olive presses. A great beam with large stones secured at one end weighed down upon the baskets filled with crushed olives. From the baskets, pure olive oil flowed down into a basin. The olive oil was then placed in jars for immediate storage.

Above: Occasionally, freshly crushed olive oil is reddish in color, as shown in this photograph in which oil pours over white rock.

Shepherd's Fields, near Bethlehem. While foraging for food, sheep occasionally stray from the flock and from their shepherd. The mortal Jesus approached a group of his followers and "was moved with compassion toward them, because they were as sheep not having a shepherd: and he began to teach them many things" (Mark 6:34).

ISAIAH 53:6

All we like sheep have gone astray; we have turned every one to his own way.

Isaiah 53 testifies again and again that Jesus Christ bore the sins of mankind. "He hath borne our griefs, and carried our sorrows," "he was wounded for our transgressions, he was bruised for our iniquities," "[he] hath laid on him the iniquity of us all," "for the transgressions of my people was he stricken," "he shall bear their iniquities," and "he bare the sin of many" (vv. 4–12).

Though Jesus Christ has carried the burdens and sins of humanity, all have strayed from the Shepherd and wandered from the strait and narrow path. Every soul who has ever lived—except for Jesus—has sinned (Romans 3:23; 1 Peter 2:25; 1 John 1:8, 10). Rather than walking the Lord's path, they often go their own way. The sheep that have strayed need a Shepherd to guide them.

ISAIAH 53:7

He is brought as a lamb to the slaughter, and as a sheep before her shearers is dumb, so he openeth not his mouth.

Isaiah uses two similes to describe Jesus Christ's atoning sacrifice: "as a lamb" and "as a sheep." Not only is Christ the Good Shepherd (John 10:14), but he is also the sacrificial lamb, who went without protest or resistance to his death. This contrasts mankind, the sheep that willfully went astray (Isaiah 53:6). The sacrifice of an unblemished lamb under the law of Moses prefigured the atoning sacrifice of Christ (Genesis 22:7–8; Exodus 12:3). The atonement fulfills the symbolism of the lamb.

The prophecy "he opened not his mouth" was fulfilled when Jesus appeared before Herod and Pilate. Herod "questioned with him in many words; but he answered him nothing" (Luke 23:9). Mark similarly records that when Jesus stood before Pilate, "the chief priests accused him of many things: but he answered nothing. And Pilate asked him again, saying, Answerest thou nothing? Behold how many things they witness against thee. But Jesus yet answered nothing" (Mark 15:3–5).

Prophetic Perfect Tense

A powerful example of the prophetic nature of the book of Isaiah is Isaiah's use of the "prophetic perfect" verb tense. With the prophetic perfect, the prophet may speak in verbs that are past, present, or future, but in every case, he is speaking of things that are yet to come. Examples are found in Isaiah 53.

Future: "For he *shall* grow up . . . when we *shall* see him" (v. 2).

Present: "He *is* despised and rejected of men" (v. 3).

Past: "We *hid* as it were our faces from him; he *was* despised" (v. 3).

Some people may be confused by the prophet's use of verbs, but he is simply using the prophetic perfect tense.

Source: Donald W. Parry, Jay A. Parry, and Tina M. Peterson, *Understanding Isaiah*, 601–2.

Above: A shepherd prepares to shear his sheep, Bethany. A sheepshearer uses special shears to cut the wool from sheep. Apparent from the scripture, the sheep's owners or their workers sheared their sheep rather than contracting that work out to others.

ISAIAH 53:9

And he made his grave with the wicked, and with the rich in his death.

Isaiah prophesies that Jesus Christ would make his "grave with the wicked." This prophecy was fulfilled when Christ was crucified between two robbers (Matthew 27:38). It may also mean that his grave was with those who had sinned, though he himself was without sin.

The prophecy that Jesus would be buried "with the rich" was fulfilled when he was buried in the tomb of the wealthy Joseph of Arimathea (Matthew 27:57–60).

ISAIAH 55:1

Ho, every one that thirsteth, come ye to the waters, and he that hath no money; come ye, buy, and eat; yea, come, buy wine and milk without money and without price.

This short passage is an invitation to come to the living waters of Christ and drink freely. Those who are thirsty are offered living water, and wine and milk besides. This promise is echoed in the Gospel of John, in which the apostle records Jesus as saying, "If any man thirst, let him come unto me, and drink" (John 7:37; Revelation 21:6; 22:17).

The living water is the love of God (1 Nephi 11:25). Ultimately, it represents Jesus Christ and his atonement, the only true source of eternal life. The blessings of the atonement have no temporal cost. Individuals pay no monetary price to receive the blessings of the atonement of Christ. Yet God does require a spiritual price: a broken heart and a contrite spirit (2 Nephi 2:7; 3 Nephi 9:20; D&C 59:8).

Above: Garden Tomb, east Jerusalem. In 1883, British General Charles Gordon suggested that the Garden Tomb area in east Jerusalem was a possible site for Christ's crucifixion and resurrection. Since that time numerous members of the Church of Jesus Christ of Latter-day Saints, as well as many other Christians, have visited and reverenced the area as a sacred site.

Below: The Dan River in northern Galilee. Just as the waters of the Dan River, the chief tributary to the Jordan River, have brought life for thousands of years to hundreds of thousands of people, so does Jesus Christ bring spiritual life to all who come to him, the living waters.

ISAIAH 64:8

But now, O Lord, thou art our father; we are the clay, and thou our potter; and we all are the work of thy hand.

Isaiah 64:8 is part of Isaiah's Intercessory Prayer, offered in powerful poetry (Isaiah 63:15–19; 64:1–12). In this prayer, the prophet pleads on behalf of his people, asking the Lord to look down from heaven in mercy (Isaiah 63:15). Isaiah directly addresses the Lord eight times—five times with the words, "O Lord," twice as "thou art our father," and once with the expression "O God."

The address, "thou art our father" (Isaiah 64:8), suggests a God who is also a Father, one who knows and loves his children. The people through Isaiah acknowledge their true relationship to their creator. As clay, they are nothing without the creator, having no shape and no power to mold themselves. They are in all things subject to the potter. It is a prayer not only from those of old but from the hearts of God's covenant people in the latter days as well.

Above: Three clay pots, Cana.

Left: A potter forms his clay. Isaiah named a number of earthly occupations and positions and symbolically identified many of them with the Lord. For example, the Lord is referred to as King (Isaiah 6:5), Counselor (Isaiah 9:6), judge (Isaiah 33:22), lawgiver (Isaiah 33:22), shepherd (Isaiah 40:11), teacher (Isaiah 48:17), and potter (Isaiah 64:8).

Mountains of Sinai.

THE RESTORATION AND THE GATHERING

Large sections of Isaiah's writings pertain to the restoration of the gospel, the gathering of Israel, and the building of Zion in the last days. Isaiah prophesied of the coming forth of the Book of Mormon, missionary work, Israel's gathering to the gospel, latter-day temples, the establishment of Zion and its stakes, and the blessings that would be enjoyed in Zion.

Nephi Affirms the Prophetic Value of Isaiah

1 Nephi 15:20

"Isaiah . . . spake concerning the restoration of the Jews, or of the house of Israel."

1 Nephi 19:23

"That I might more fully persuade them to believe in the Lord their Redeemer I did read unto them that which was written by the prophet Isaiah."

1 Nephi 19:24

"Hear ye the words of the prophet, which were written unto all the house of Israel."

2 Nephi 6:4

"Behold, I would speak unto you concerning things . . . which are to come; wherefore, I will read you the words of Isaiah."

2 Nephi 6:4

"I speak [the words of Isaiah] . . . that ye may learn and glorify the name of your God."

2 Nephi 11:2

"[Isaiah] verily saw my Redeemer."

2 Nephi 11:8

"And now I write some of the words of Isaiah, that whoso of my people shall see these words may lift up their hearts and rejoice for all men."

2 Nephi 11:8

"And ye may liken [the words of Isaiah] unto you and unto all men."

2 Nephi 25:4

"The words of Isaiah . . . are plain unto all those that are filled with the spirit of prophecy."

2 Nephi 25:5

"Yea, and my soul delighteth in the words of Isaiah."

2 Nephi 25:7–8

"The prophecies of Isaiah . . . are of great worth unto them in the last days."

ISAIAH 2:2–3

And it shall come to pass in the last days, that the mountain of the Lord's house shall be established in the top of the mountains, and shall be exalted above the hills; and all nations shall flow unto it. . . . and he will teach us of his ways, and we will walk in his paths.

Isaiah speaks directly to members of the Church of Jesus Christ of Latter-day Saints today. Many are blessed to see the fulfillment of this prophecy as they enter the Lord's temples and are taught of "his ways" and walk in "his paths." Isaiah's prophecy of the "mountain of the Lord" is fulfilled as temples are built throughout the world (Isaiah 2:1–5).

The prophecy ultimately refers to the Salt Lake Temple, nestled in the hills and mountains, as well as to the future temple of Jerusalem, which will be established in the mountains of Judea (v. 1). People from all nations will gather to obey the God of all nations and to help build up his kingdom on earth. Joseph Smith taught that "there should be a place where all nations shall come up from time to time to receive their endowments" (*Teachings of the Prophet Joseph Smith*, 367; see also 27).

For a gathering of people to "flow," as a river up a mountain, a power greater than gravity must be at work. This power is the power of God and of the temple. Joseph Smith summed up the connection between this latter-day gathering of Israel and temple service: "The object of gathering the Jews, or the people of God in any age of the world . . . was to build unto the Lord a house whereby He could reveal unto His people the ordinances of His house and the glories of His kingdom, and teach the people the way of salvation" (*History of the Church*, 5:423).

Right: The Salt Lake Temple stands near the foothills of the Wasatch Mountains. Its soaring pinnacles and peaks recall the holy mountains of ancient times. This great temple, which hundreds of thousands have visited, partially fulfills Isaiah's prophecy that "all nations shall flow" to "the mountain of the Lord's house."

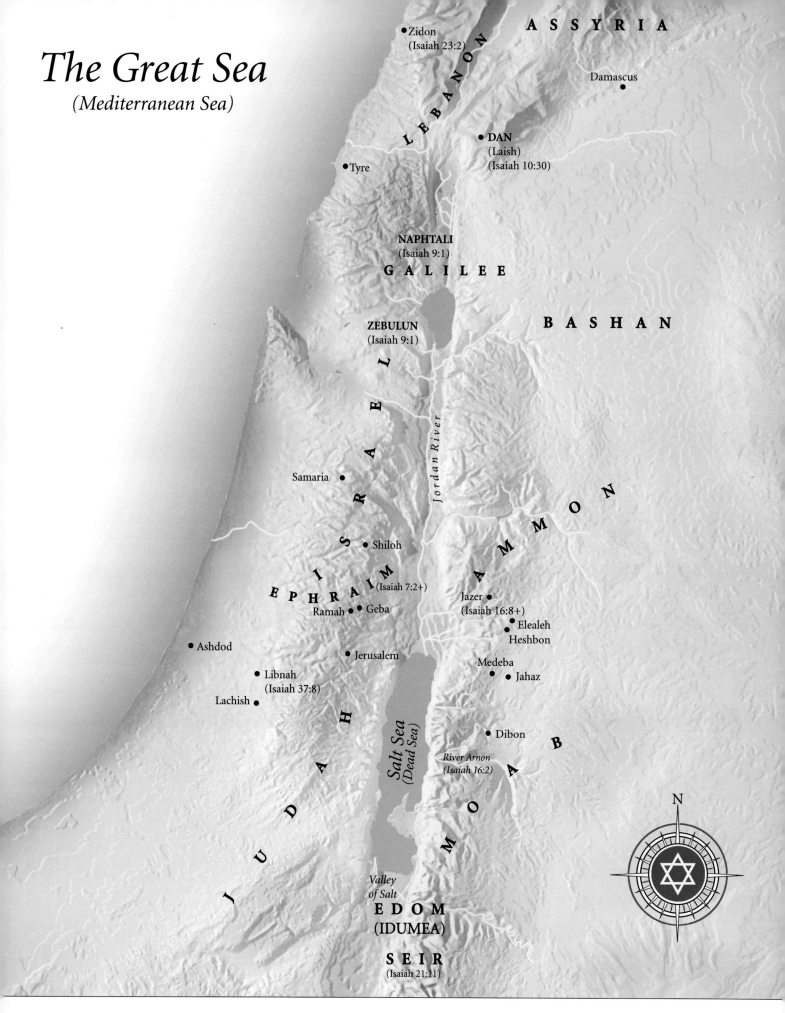

The Great Sea
(Mediterranean Sea)

ASSYRIA

Zidon
(Isaiah 23:2)

Damascus

LEBANON

DAN
(Laish)
(Isaiah 10:30)

Tyre

NAPHTALI
(Isaiah 9:1)

GALILEE

BASHAN

ZEBULUN
(Isaiah 9:1)

Jordan River

Samaria

ISRAEL

AMMON

Shiloh

EPHRAIM
(Isaiah 7:2+)

Jazer
(Isaiah 16:8+)

Ramah   Geba

Elealeh
Heshbon

Ashdod

Jerusalem

Medeba
Jahaz

Libnah
(Isaiah 37:8)

Lachish

JUDAH

Dibon

Salt Sea
(Dead Sea)

River Arnon
(Isaiah 16:2)

M O A B

N

*Valley
of Salt*

EDOM
(IDUMEA)

SEIR
(Isaiah 21:11)

**The Kingdoms of Israel and Judah and Surrounding Regions
at the Time of Isaiah**

ISAIAH 5:30

And in that day they shall roar against them like the roaring of the sea.

Isaiah 5:26–30 introduces two divine activities that will attract members of the house of Israel to their lands of promise in the last days. One, God will hold up a flag, or standard, to all the nations of the earth around which Israel will rally. And two, God will attract the attention of Israel through a "hiss," sometimes translated from Hebrew as "whistle."

In the context of these two divine activities, verse 30 seems to suggest that the children of Zion shall roar like the roaring of the sea. They will be armed with the Spirit and its gifts. They will possess great priesthood powers that are mightier than the great roaring of the earth's oceans.

ISAIAH 10:22

For though thy people Israel be as the sand of the sea, yet a remnant of them shall return.

Isaiah 10:20–27 pertains to scattered Israel's return to its lands of promise and the renewal of its covenant status with God in the last days. The Old Testament formula for an apostate people's return to God is found in 2 Chronicles 30:6–9. These verses speak of Israel's return to the promised land, to God through repentance, and to true temple worship. The expression "as the sands of the sea" recalls the Abrahamic covenant that speaks of Abraham's posterity becoming as numerous as the sands of the sea (Genesis 22:17; Abraham 3:14). Although the number of children of Israel will be exceedingly high, only a remnant will return.

Above: The roaring waves of the Mediterranean Sea, near Akko. In the Old Testament, the Mediterranean Sea is called the Great Sea because of its great size compared to the Dead Sea and the Sea of Galilee. It is also called the Western Sea because it lies west of the Holy Land. It stretches west from the coastline approximately 2100 miles to Gibraltar. Biblical coastal cities on its shores included Sidon, Tyre, Akko, Joppa, Ashdod, and Ashkelon.

Below: Sand dunes on the Mediterranean seashore, near Gaza. The great stretch of sandy seashore next to the Mediterranean Sea together with the immense deserts of sand throughout the Near East have made sand the subject of many similes in the scriptures.

ISAIAH 11:6

The wolf also shall dwell with the lamb, and the leopard shall lie down with the kid; and the calf and the young lion and the fatling together; and a little child shall lead them.

This passage speaks of the millennium. Old enmities and hostilities will cease, signaling a change in the order of things. Six animals are listed. The wolf, leopard, and lion are wild beasts that typically feed on the lamb, kid, and calf, which are domestic animals. The wild animals, ferocious predators, are a threat to mankind. The tame animals are docile, submissive, nonthreatening, and useful to humanity.

Isaiah 11:6 may be taken literally. Harmony in nature will characterize the millennial period of earth's history. The phrase "a little child shall lead them" suggests that small children will not only feel safe among ferocious beasts but will have control over them and lead them (Isaiah 11:6–9). "The enmity of beasts, yea, the enmity of all flesh, shall cease" (D&C 101:26).

The passage is also symbolic. The wolf, leopard, and lion represent those who foment war and murder. The lamb, kid, and calf symbolize meek and peaceful people. All will dwell together in peace during the millennium.

Above top: Leopard, Hai-Bar Yotvata Nature Reserve. The leopard, a spotted cat found in the Holy Land, feeds on lambs and other small animals, thus posing a threat to the livelihood of shepherds.

Above middle: Six goat kids foraging on a hillside near Bethel. Domesticated goats served many useful purposes to Old Testament peoples, providing meat, milk, leather, and goat-hair for cloth and tents. The kids were especially valued as food. Goats, unlike cattle, were able to feed on moderately barren ground. They were easy prey for carnivorous beasts.

Right: A boy waves to passersby in Jerusalem.

ISAIAH 18:3

All ye inhabitants of the world, and dwellers on the earth, see ye, when he lifteth up an ensign on the mountains; and when he bloweth a trumpet, hear ye.

Isaiah identifies two symbols—the ensign and the trumpet—that invite earth's inhabitants in the latter days to gather to the Lord's church and kingdom.

On three occasions the ram's horn, often translated "trumpet," is mentioned in the writings of Isaiah (Isaiah 18:3; 27:13; 58:1). The trumpet's sound is clear, loud, and unmistakable. It beckons the world's inhabitants to gather to the gospel (Isaiah 27:13; Matthew 24:31). Every missionary of this dispensation is instructed that "at all times, and in all places, he shall open his mouth and declare my gospel as with the voice of a trump" (D&C 24:12) so that the earth's inhabitants may hear the gospel's message.

Isaiah also speaks concerning an ensign—or banner or flag—that would be erected upon a mountain (Isaiah 5:26; 11:10–12; 18:3; 30:17; 31:9; 49:22). In the latter days the ensign is a highly visible symbol that represents the gospel of Jesus Christ (see D&C 45:9; 105:39) and the light that accompanies it (D&C 115:4–5).

Two Millennial Hymns

The righteous will sing these two hymns from Isaiah 12 during the millennium (see the chapter heading for Isaiah 12). The first hymn focuses on the Lord and his salvation. The second hymn conveys that the Lord is "exalted" and "great." In both hymns, the righteous praise the Lord because of all the wonderful things he has done for his people.

And in that day thou shalt say,

O Lord, I will praise thee:
though thou wast angry with me,
thine anger is turned away, and thou comfortest me.
Behold, God is my salvation;
I will trust, and not be afraid:
for the Lord Jehovah is my strength and my song;
he also is become my salvation.
Therefore with joy shall ye draw water out of the wells of salvation.

And in that day shall ye say,

Praise the Lord, call upon his name,
declare his doings among the people,
make mention that his name is exalted.
Sing unto the Lord;
for he hath done excellent things: this is known in all the earth.
Cry out and shout, thou inhabitant of Zion:
for great is the Holy One of Israel in the midst of thee.

Left: A man, standing near the Western Wall, Jerusalem, blows a ram's horn. The ceremonial ram's horn was called a shofar, often translated "trumpet" in the King James Version of the Bible. It was sounded during various military and religious occasions. For instance, Psalm 150:1, 3 reads: "Praise ye the Lord. Praise God in his sanctuary . . . . Praise him with the sound of the trumpet: praise him with the psaltery and harp."

For in that day every man shall cast away his idols of silver, and his idols of gold, which your own hands have made unto you for a sin.

Isaiah 31:4–9 speaks mainly to people of the latter days. If those who are part of Zion will cast away their wickedness as one casts away false gods, then the Lord will defend Zion. He will be like a mighty lion, "roaring on his prey" (v. 4), or like a bird, flying protectively over its nestlings to preserve them (v. 5). He will use his mighty sword to protect Zion (v. 8). In verse 7, Isaiah prophesies once again that one day the people of Israel will cease their worship of false gods (see Isaiah 30:22 for a similar prophecy).

Top: These four idols are examples of those worshiped in ancient Israel. Idols were generally made of three materials: stone, metal, and wood. Wooden idols were often carved from a log and then covered with plaster or a thin layer of metal.

Middle right: White blossoms in the wilderness south of Sedom. The scenes call to mind Isaiah's prophecy that "the desert shall rejoice, and blossom as a rose."

Bottom right: The blossoms of an almond tree in Neot Kedumim, a biblical landscape reserve. The almond tree is the first of fruit trees to blossom after or even during the winter months, flowering as early as January. Perhaps for this reason, the almond is called in Hebrew *shaked,* or "waker." The tree with its blossoms was of sufficient beauty and import that the temple menorah (candlestick) was ornamented with designs of almonds and blossoms. "And in the candlestick shall be four bowls made like unto almonds, with their knops and their flowers" (Exodus 25:31–37).

ISAIAH 35:1–2

The wilderness and the solitary place shall be glad for them; and the desert shall rejoice, and blossom as the rose. It shall blossom abundantly.

Isaiah compares the blossoming of the desert, or wilderness, to the righteous of latter-day Israel. This includes the Lamanites, who are like flowers in the desert that blossom abundantly. Elsewhere Isaiah writes, "Israel shall blossom and bud, and fill the face of the world with fruit" (Isaiah 27:6; D&C 33:5).

Modern revelation adds light to the passage of Isaiah cited above: "But before the great day of the Lord shall come, Jacob shall flourish in the wilderness, and the Lamanites shall blossom as the rose. Zion shall flourish upon the hills and rejoice upon the mountains" (D&C 49:24–25). The revelation places Jacob in the "wilderness," a term also used in Isaiah 35, and readers learn that Jacob and Zion shall "flourish" and the Lamanites shall "blossom." The words "flourish" and "blossom" suggest that Jacob, Zion, and the Lamanites are like plants or flowers that will thrive spiritually.

After the death of Jesus and his apostles, the church was driven "into the wilderness" (D&C 86:3), but the restoration of the gospel has caused "the coming forth of [the Lord's] church out of the wilderness" (D&C 5:14). The house of Israel is becoming more spiritual.

Plant Terms

barley	28:25	herb(s)	18:4; 26:19
berries	17:6	leaf/leaves	1:30; 34:4
blossom	5:24; 27:6	myrtle	41:19; 55:13
bough(s)	10:33; 17:6	nettles	34:13
box tree	41:19; 60:13	oak(s)	1:30; 6:13
brambles	34:13	olive	17:6; 24:13
branch(es)	4:2; 9:14	pine	41:19; 60:13
brier(s)	5:6; 7:23	plant(s)	5:7; 17:10
bud	18:5; 27:6	reed(s)	19:6–7
bulrush(es)	18:2; 58:5	rie (rye)	28:25
bushes	7:19	root	5:24; 11:10
cane	43:24	rose	35:1
cedar(s)	2:13; 9:10	rush	9:14; 19:15
chaff	5:24; 17:13	seed	5:10; 6:13
corn	17:5	shittah	41:19
cucumbers	1:8	sprigs	18:5
cummin	28:25, 27	stem	11:1
cypress	44:14	stock	40:24; 44:19
fig(s)	36:16; 38:21	straw	11:7; 25:10
fir	14:8; 37:24	stubble	5:24; 33:11
fitches	28:25, 27	sycomores	9:10
flower	18:5; 28:1	teil tree	6:13
forest	9:18; 10:18	thickets	9:18; 10:34
fruit(s)	3:10; 4:2	thorn(s)	5:6; 7:19
grape(s)	5:2; 18:5	tree(s)	6:13; 44:23
grass	15:6; 35:7	vine(s)	5:2; 16:8
harvest	9:3; 16:9	vineyard(s)	1:8; 5:1
hay	15:6	wheat	28:25
hedge	5:5	willows	15:7; 44:4

Right: The wilderness of Judah is a dry and rocky wasteland that does not support much plant life. During the biblical era it was basically uninhabitable except by nomadic peoples who occupied it on occasions when the land yielded scant forage for their flocks.

Above: Reeds and rushes at En Gedi. These water-loving plants thrive on the banks of pools and streams. They were useful to humans in a variety of ways: as measuring rods, writing instruments, fuel, and material for baskets, small skiffs, rope, and paper.

Below: Parched earth near Sedom, the southern end of the Dead Sea. According to a prophecy of Isaiah, parched ground will one day have pools of water.

ISAIAH 35:6–7

For in the wilderness shall waters break out, and streams in the desert. And the parched ground shall become a pool, and the thirsty land springs of water: in the habitation of dragons, where each lay, shall be grass with reeds and rushes.

These two verses continue the prophecy in Isaiah 35:1–2 that "the desert shall rejoice, and blossom as the rose. It shall blossom abundantly." Before the restoration of the gospel, the house of Israel was like a "wilderness" and "parched earth." But with the restoration and its great blessings, powers, and glories, those members of the house of Israel who have gathered to the church have blossomed because of the "waters" and "streams in the desert," "pools" of water in parched ground, and "springs of water" in a land that is thirsty.

Through the power of Christ, desolate wastelands will become gardens in the last days. The waters point to Christ and his salvation. Earlier Isaiah wrote that the "Lord will be unto us a place of broad rivers and streams" (Isaiah 33:21).

Reeds and rushes require ample water and cannot grow in the harsh wilderness. These plants probably represent the righteous who partake of the waters of life.

ISAIAH 40:9

O Zion, that bringest good tidings, get thee up into the high mountain; O Jerusalem, that bringest good tidings, lift up thy voice with strength; lift it up, be not afraid; say unto the cities of Judah, Behold your God!

Isaiah calls out to Zion and Jerusalem to prepare for the coming of their Lord. Before Zion's messengers take the restored gospel, or "good tidings," to the world, they are commanded to go up to the high mountain, or God's temple. Isaiah's words apply to Latter-day Saints. "Ye are sent forth . . . to teach the children of men the things which I have put into your hands by the power of my Spirit; and ye are to be taught from on high. Sanctify yourselves and ye shall be endowed with power" (D&C 43:15–16; 110:9).

The good news of the Lord's gospel will go forth from Jerusalem to the cities of Judah, or to all of the lands where the children of Judah dwell, to call them to come and behold their God. In a broader sense, Zion and Jerusalem stand as a symbol for all the covenant people of God.

Above: Mountain and camels in the Negev desert. When temple buildings did not exist upon the earth, the prophets sometimes worshiped on high mountains, including Mount Sinai, Mount Moriah, and the Mount of Transfiguration. Many prophets have compared mountains to temples. Isaiah, too, uses language that seems to equate mountains and temples. Both figure prominently on the landscape, and both are places set apart from the regular pursuits of mortality.

How Firm a Foundation

Some of the words of the hymn "How Firm a Foundation" are adapted from Isaiah 41:10.

Fear not, I am with thee;
Oh, be not dismayed,
For I am thy God
And will still give thee aid.
I'll strengthen thee, help thee,
and cause thee to stand,
Upheld by my righteous,
Omnipotent hand.

Source: Text attributed to Robert Keen, ca. 1787, *Hymns,* no. 85.

Above: Threshing floor, Neot Kedumim, a biblical landscape reserve. A threshing floor that receives prominent mention in the Old Testament is the one that belonged to Araunah the Jebusite before it was sold to King David (2 Samuel 24:18–25). That threshing floor became the site of the temple at Jerusalem. Typical threshing floors were located on large, flat surfaces, usually rock outcroppings or packed earth. Ideally, a threshing floor was situated on a hill exposed to a breeze so that chaff, when separated from grain kernels, would be blown away.

Below: Threshing wheat with a primitive sledge, Salamant, Egypt's Delta. One type of threshing instrument consisted of thick planks attached together, with perforations that held teeth made from sharp pieces of basaltic rock or iron. The instrument was drawn over grain by powerful beasts while the teeth separated kernels from straw. Subsequently, harvesters prepared the grain and straw for winnowing.

ISAIAH 41:15

Behold, I will make thee a new sharp threshing instrument having teeth: thou shalt thresh the mountains, and beat them small, and shalt make the hills as chaff.

Isaiah 41:1–20 pertains to the Lord blessing Israel, his servant. Isaiah's prophetic promises to Israel are wonderful. They have application to the Lord's servants in the latter days.

Verse 15 says that God will mold the righteous of the last days into a powerful threshing instrument, enabling them to perform their work of gathering souls to Christ. In Isaiah's time, a threshing instrument was dragged over grain by an ox or ass to separate the grain kernels from the husks. To help the house of Israel fulfill its mission, which is often compared to harvesting, the Lord will make it into a new threshing instrument. Most threshing instruments work best on level ground, but this threshing tool, created by the Lord, has special capabilities. It threshes hills and mountains, a seemingly impossible task. That means that the house of Israel will be capable of performing remarkable works through the power of God. Though they are "the weak things of the world, those who are unlearned and despised," God has called upon them "to thrash the nations by the power of [his] Spirit" (D&C 35:13).

Part of the goal in harvesting the white fields is to seek out the honest in heart (D&C 4). Eventually the righteous will be separated from the wicked, just as wheat is separated from the tares (Isaiah 41:16). For other uses of the images of threshing, threshing instruments, or threshing floors in Isaiah, see 21:10; 27:12; 28:23–29; 41:15.

ISAIAH 41:18

I will open rivers in high places, and fountains in the midst of the valleys: I will make the wilderness a pool of water, and the dry land springs of water.

In Isaiah 41, Isaiah addresses a number of issues that concern members of the Church of Jesus Christ of Latter-day Saints. The Lord has said, "[they] are the children of Israel" (D&C 103:17). Isaiah says that, as part of Israel,

they are God's servants (Isaiah 41:8);

they are his chosen people (v. 9);

they are called by God from among the chief men of the earth (v. 9);

they are to fear not, for God will strengthen, help, and uphold them (v. 10).

The Lord also promises that

while holding their right hand, he will say, "Fear not; I will help thee" (v. 13);

he will mold them into powerful, unique instruments, enabling them to perform their work (vv. 15–16);

those who are against them will be ashamed and confounded and will perish (v. 11);

those who war against them will be "as nothing, and as a thing of nought" (v. 12).

If the children of Israel are ever thirsty, physically or spiritually, their small, empty cups will never suffice. God desires to give them a great river full of water to fill their needs. He says, "I will open rivers . . . and fountains . . . and . . . springs of water" (v. 18). Such are the great promises to the house of Israel.

Above: Flowing stream, below Banias Falls. Banias is a tributary that helps form the Jordan River. In Isaiah's time, as well as in the modern era, Banias provided essential water to civilization.

Right: The Dan River, near Tel Dan. This is the Jordan River's major source of water, originating from Mount Hermon's melting snows. The Jordan River runs through the Sea of Galilee and southward into the Dead Sea. Most of the Jordan flows below sea level, making it the world's lowest river. The river has regularly played an important geopolitical role among nations and kingdoms. During the Israelite period it formed a geographical division between the eastern and western tribes of Israel.

Above: Modern quivers, Old City, Jerusalem. An archer generally carried his quiver on his back with the arrows near his right shoulder, making them easily accessible. The quiver, usually made of leather or wood, "hid" and thus protected the arrows.

ISAIAH 49:2

And [the Lord] hath made my mouth like a sharp sword; in the shadow of his hand hath he hid me, and made me a polished shaft; in his quiver hath he hid me.

Joseph Smith referred to this prophecy in relation to himself: "I am like a huge, rough stone rolling down from a high mountain; and the only polishing I get is when some corner gets rubbed off by coming in contact with something else, striking with accelerated force against religious bigotry, priestcraft, . . . corrupt men and women—all hell knocking off a corner here and a corner there. Thus I will become a smooth and polished shaft in the quiver of the Almighty" (*Teachings of the Prophet Joseph Smith*, 304).

The Lord, through Isaiah, uses symbols to refer to his power in his follower's lives. "Mouth like a sharp sword" refers to the power of the message brought by God's servant. It is an expression common in revelation. Hebrews 4:12, for example, reads, "For the word of God is quick, and powerful, and sharper than any two-edged sword, piercing even to the dividing asunder of soul and spirit, and of the joints and marrow, and is a discerner of the thoughts and intents of the heart" (see also Revelation 1:16; D&C 6:2).

The two phrases "shadow of his hand" and "in his quiver" refer to God's divine protection. The shadow of God's hand is a place of ultimate safety (Isaiah 51:16). Arrows stored in an archer's quiver are protected from the elements and always at hand. Similarly, God's people receive his divine protection from both physical and spiritual harm. Through God's power, his people are like the "polished shaft" of an arrow, fully prepared to accomplish his mission.

Names of Body Parts

arm	9:20; 49:22	eye(s)	13:18; 52:8	loins	11:5; 20:2
back	38:17; 50:5	face(s)	3:15; 6:2	marrow	25:6
beard	7:20	feet	3:16	mouth(s)	1:20; 52:15
belly	46:3	finger	58:9	neck(s)	8:8; 10:27
blood	1:11, 15	flesh	22:13; 31:3	nose	3:21; 37:29
bones	38:13; 58:11	hair	3:24; 7:20	palms	49:16
bowels	16:11; 48:19	hand	1:12, 15	shoulder(s)	9:4, 6
breast(s)	60:16; 66:11	head(s)	15:2; 35:10	sole(s)	1:6; 37:25
brow	48:4	heart(s)	1:5; 44:18	teeth	41:15
buttocks	20:4	kidneys	34:6	thigh	47:2
cheeks	50:6	knee(s)	35:3; 66:12	tongue(s)	3:8; 11:15
crown of the head	3:17	leg(s)	3:20; 47:2	womb	13:18; 44:2
ear(s)	1:2; 5:9	lips	6:5, 7		

ISAIAH 49:18

Lift up thine eyes round about, and behold: all these gather themselves together, and come to thee. As I live, saith the Lord, thou shalt surely clothe thee with them all, as with an ornament, and bind them on thee, as a bride doeth.

In Isaiah 49:13–21, the Lord comforts his returning children as they gather in the last days. In verse 18, the Lord, depicted as the bridegroom, speaks to latter-day Israel, or the church, depicted as the bride. (See Isaiah 61:10; D&C 109:73–74; Revelation 21:2 for other examples of bride and groom symbolism.) The Lord tells his bride to look around and see all of the children coming to her. Then, using symbolic language, he promises her that she will clothe herself with many children, just as a bride wears many ornaments and jewelry at her wedding.

In this verse, then, the bride's ornaments represent those who become Zion. As additional souls are gathered unto Zion, they will add to the glory of those already there. As fine clothing or expensive jewelry are precious to a bride, so are the souls of those gathered to the church.

Family and Relationship Terms

babes	3:4
bride	49:18; 61:10; 62:5
bridegroom	61:10; 62:5
brother	3:6; 9:19
child(ren)	3:5; 7:16
daughter(s)	1:8; 10:30
father(s)	3:6; 8:4
firstborn	14:30
husband	54:5
infant	65:20
mother	8:4; 49:1
nephew	14:22
son(s)	1:1; 37:38
widow(s)	1:17, 23
wife/wives	54:1, 6

Above right: Bracelets, Israel Museum. It is the custom of many Near Eastern cultures, both modern and ancient, for a bride to adorn herself with jewels and ornaments at her wedding. Isaiah speaks of the "bride [who] adorneth herself with her jewels" (Isaiah 61:10). If a bride was unable to purchase jewelry, she borrowed it from family or friends. Various types of jewelry—necklaces, bracelets, earrings, finger rings, crowns—have been discovered in archaeological digs throughout biblical lands.

Below right: A Bedouin woman dressed in traditional clothing and decked with jewelry.

Enlarge the place of thy tent, and let them stretch forth the curtains of thine habitations: spare not, lengthen thy cords, and strengthen thy stakes.

One ecclesiastical division of the Church of Jesus Christ of Latter-day Saints is a stake. Tent stakes, or pegs, help hold up and enlarge a tent. Each stake must be strong to keep the tent stable. President Ezra Taft Benson wrote, "To members, the term *stake* is a symbolic expression. Picture in your mind a great tent held up by cords extended to many stakes that are firmly secured in the ground. The prophets likened latter-day Zion to a great tent encompassing the earth. That tent was supported by cords fastened to stakes (3 Nephi 22:2; Isaiah 54:2). Those stakes, of course, are various geographical organizations spread out over the earth. Presently Israel is being gathered to the various stakes of Zion" (*Come unto Christ,* 101).

The five commands in Isaiah 54:2, "enlarge," "stretch forth," "spare not," "lengthen," and "strengthen," teach church members what they should be doing to build Zion in these last days (see also Moroni 10:31; D&C 133:9). One way that Zion will enlarge its tent and strengthen its stakes is to practice the law of consecration (D&C 82:12–15).

Below: Bedouin tents were made of goat-hair cloth, sewn and patched together. The horizontal covering was stretched over a series of poles, and the ends were secured to the ground with tent stakes. Vertical hangings were used both for protection from the elements as well as for interior divisions, creating "rooms." The tent could be enlarged by weaving additional cloth to the covering, lengthening the cords, and strengthening the stakes. Bedouin tents are still used today and may be seen in many parts of the Near East.

For ye shall go out with joy, and be led forth with peace: the mountains and the hills shall break forth before you into singing, and all the trees of the field shall clap their hands.

As Israel is gathered to the gospel of Jesus Christ and to its lands of inheritance in the last days, it will come forth in joy and peace. The gathering in joy and peace greatly contrasts the exodus from Egypt, which was fraught with fear and turmoil (Exodus 5–14; Isaiah 52:12). Joy and peace are two of the most desired fruits of the Spirit (Romans 14:17; Galatians 5:22). They are also the two primary messages of the gospel. "Whoso shall publish peace, yea, tidings of great joy, how beautiful upon the mountains shall they be" (1 Nephi 13:37). Joy comes from having received a remission of sins (Mosiah 4:3).

Even nature will join in the rejoicing as the children of Israel gather—the mountains and hills will sing and the trees will clap their hands. Elsewhere Isaiah records the manner in which the natural world will rejoice when the Lord redeems Israel: "Sing, O ye heavens; for the Lord hath done it: shout, ye lower parts of the earth: break forth into singing, ye mountains, O forest, and every tree therein: for the Lord hath redeemed Jacob, and glorified himself in Israel" (Isaiah 44:23). Also, "Sing, O heavens; and be joyful, O earth; and break forth into singing, O mountains: for the Lord hath comforted his people, and will have mercy upon his afflicted" (Isaiah 49:13; 1 Chronicles 16:33).

Above: Palm tree beside the Sea of Galilee. Palms are common to parts of the Holy Land. Some types produce delicious fruit, and their branches symbolize victory and rejoicing (John 12:13). The Psalmist taught, "The righteous shall flourish like the palm tree" (Psalm 92:12).

Right: The remains of Nimrod's Castle, a structure from the Crusader period, stand on this mountain. The mountain is near Caesarea Philippi.

Animal Terms

asp	11:8
ass(es)	21:7; 30:6
bats	2:20
bear(s)	11:7; 59:11
beast(s)	35:9; 43:20
bee	7:18
bird(s)	16:2; 46:11
bittern	14:23; 34:11
bull(s)/bullock(s)	1:11; 34:7
calf	11:6; 27:10
camels	21:7; 30:6
caterpillar	33:4
cattle	7:25; 30:23
cockatrice	11:8; 14:29
cormorant	34:11
cow	7:21; 11:7
crane	38:14
dogs	56:10–11
dove(s)	38:14; 60:8
dromedaries	60:6
eagle(s)	40:31
fish	19:10; 50:2
fly	7:18
fold	13:20; 65:10
fowls	18:6
goats	1:11; 34:6
grasshoppers	40:22
hart	35:6
heifer	15:5
herds	65:10
horse(s)	43:17; 63:13
kid	11:6
lamb(s)	11:6; 16:1
leopard	11:6
leviathan	27:1
lion(s)	5:29; 11:6
locusts	33:4
moles	2:20
moth	50:9; 51:8
mouse	66:17
mules	66:20
owl(s)	34:11, 14
ox(en)	1:3; 11:7
rams	1:11; 34:6
raven	34:11
roe	13:14
satyr	34:14
serpent	14:29; 27:1
sheep	7:21; 13:14
spider	59:5
swine	65:4; 66:3
unicorns	34:7
viper	30:6; 59:5
vultures	34:15
wolf	11:6; 65:25
worm(s)	14:11; 41:14

ISAIAH 60:6–7

The multitude of camels shall cover thee, the dromedaries of Midian and Ephah; all they from Sheba shall come: they shall bring gold and incense; and they shall shew forth the praises of the Lord. All the flocks of Kedar shall be gathered together unto thee, the rams of Nebaioth shall minister unto thee.

In the last days Zion will be established, shining like a light to the world. The glory of the Lord will be there, and many will seek to join themselves to it, bringing their wealth with them. (See Isaiah 60:1–22 for a full description of this time.) The gentiles will add much wealth and strength to Israel, symbolized by the terms "forces," "multitude of camels," "dromedaries of Midian and Ephah," "gold," "incense," "flocks of Kedar," "rams of Nebaioth," "ships of Tarshish," "silver," and "glory of Lebanon" (vv. 5–13).

During the biblical period, wealth could be measured by the number of camels and flocks a family possessed. Similarly, the animals mentioned above symbolize much wealth that will be brought to Zion in the last days. Not only will the gentiles gather to Zion, but they will also carry many riches with them. The many references to wealth may also refer to spiritual gifts and treasures.

Below: Camel, Bedouin camp, Sinai Peninsula. Camels were an important means of transportation for many of the ancients, including Abraham and Jacob. The animals are able to travel great distances through the desert, while carrying their own internal supply of water. They are capable of carrying heavy loads of goods and can travel up to ten miles an hour.

ISAIAH 66:20

And they shall bring all your brethren for an offering unto the Lord out of all nations . . . to my holy mountain Jerusalem, saith the Lord, as the children of Israel bring an offering in a clean vessel into the house of the Lord.

In preparation for the second coming and the millennium, the Lord will gather the righteous from all nations (Isaiah 66:18). Missionaries will go forth to declare his glory among the gentiles, even to far-off places that do not know the true God (v. 19). The missionaries will bring the gentile converts to the temple, or holy mountain, as an offering unto the Lord (v. 20). The offering may be the souls of converts, with the clean vessel being their pure bodies, or it may be the names of the dead they bring to the temple for vicarious ordinance work (D&C 128:24). The gentiles will be granted the privilege of holding the priesthood and of participating in temple worship (Isaiah 66:21).

Above and right: Clean vessels for offerings, Temple Museum, Jewish Quarter, Jerusalem. Various vessels were required for the operation of the temple and its rituals. Bowls, dishes, and other types of containers (Exodus 25:29) stored or received olive oil, incense, and sacrificial blood at the altar. The vessels used in the temple had to be ritually clean, for their offerings were presented to the Lord.

Chiasmus

Chiasmus is an inverted parallelism, a presentation of a series of words or thoughts followed by a second presentation of a series of words or thoughts but in reverse order. In the following examples, the As parallel one another, as do the Bs, Cs, and so on.

For example, in Isaiah 6:10, the word "heart" is found in the two A lines, the word "ears" is found in the two B lines, and "eyes" is found in the two C lines. The chiasmus, then, features the words "heart," "ears," "eyes," "eyes," "ears," and "heart."

Isaiah 6:10

  A Make the heart of this people fat,
    B and make their ears heavy,
      C and shut their eyes;
      C lest they see with their eyes,
    B and hear with their ears,
  A and understand with their heart, and convert, and be healed.

Isaiah 55:8–9

  A For my thoughts are not your thoughts,
    B neither are your ways my ways, saith the Lord.
      C For as the heavens are higher
      C than the earth,
    B so are my ways higher than your ways,
  A and my thoughts than your thoughts.

Isaiah 60:1–3

  A Arise,
    B shine;
      C for thy light is come,
        D and the glory
          E of the Lord
            F is risen upon thee.
              G For, behold, the darkness shall cover the earth,
              G and gross darkness the people:
            F but shall arise upon thee,
          E the Lord
        D and his glory shall be seen upon thee,
      C and the nations shall come to thy light
    B and kings to the brightness
  A of thy rising.

Translation by Donald W. Parry

THE SECOND COMING OF JESUS CHRIST

Many of Isaiah's prophecies pertain to the last days, the second coming, and the millennial reign of Jesus Christ. These prophecies foretell that Jesus the Messiah will smite the earth and slay the wicked at his coming, preparing the way for the glorious millennium, when he will rule with justice and righteousness. Isaiah wrote using images from his time that still carry this powerful message to people today.

View of the skyscape over the Judean hills.

They shall beat their swords into plowshares, and their spears into pruninghooks: nation shall not lift up sword against nation, neither shall they learn war any more.

The passage refers to the millennium, when peace will prevail. Instruments of destruction will be transformed into instruments of production. The instruments Isaiah mentions, swords, spears, plowshares, and pruning hooks, all have blades. Swords and spears are instruments that represent war and destruction (2 Nephi 1:18; 3 Nephi 2:19; D&C 45:33). Plowshares and pruning hooks represent peace and prosperity. A plowshare is the cutting blade of a plow. A pruning hook is a tool with a hooked blade that is used for pruning plants.

During the millennium nations will not participate in war, for they will destroy their weapons, making them into useful implements. Isaiah says that the nations will not even "learn war" any more.

Above: A pruning hook is a knifelike instrument with a short, broad blade used for pruning vines and harvesting grapes. Isaiah describes the pruning process: "For afore the harvest, when the bud is perfect, . . . he shall both cut off the sprigs with pruning hooks, and take away and cut down the branches" (Isaiah 18:5).

Above: Plowshares without the plow, Neot Kedumim, a biblical landscape reserve.

Left: Cave north of Qumran. Hundreds of natural caves exist in the central hill country of Judea and Samaria as well as in the deserts and fault escarpment overlooking the Dead Sea region. In ancient times, caves served as hiding places, dwellings, and tombs.

ISAIAH 2:10

Enter into the rock, and hide thee in the dust, for fear of the Lord, and for the glory of his majesty.

At the great and dreadful day of the Lord, or the second coming, wicked people will attempt to hide from the Lord and his glory. They may literally hide in rocks or caves or they may try to hide their wrongs from God. Their attempt to hide will be in vain because the Lord's power and great glory illuminate everything.

Revelation 6:15 presents a scenario similar to that found in Isaiah 2:10: "And the kings of the earth, and the great men, and the rich men, and the chief captains, and the mighty men, and every bondman, and every free man, hid themselves in the dens and in the rocks of the mountains" because they feared the Lord.

Representative List of Isaiah Quotations, Paraphrases, or Allusions in Modern Latter-day Revelations in the Doctrine and Covenants

Isaiah	Doctrine and Covenants
1:2	76:1
1:18	45:10; 50:10–12
1:19	64:34
2:2–3	133:12–13
4:5	45:63–75; 84:5
4:6	115:6
5:1–7	101:43–62
8:16	88:84; 133:72
11:1–5	113:1–4
11:4	19:15
11:10	113:5–6
11:16	133:26–29
13:1	133:14
13:10	29:14; 34:9; 45:42; 88:87
13:13	133:49
14:12	21:6; 35:24
24:5	76:26
24:20	1:15
25:6	49:23; 88:87
28:10	58:8
28:15, 18	98:12; 128:21
28:21	45:31; 5:19; 97:23
29:14	95:4; 101:95; 4:1; 6:1; 11:1; 12:1; 14:1; 18:44
33:22	76:9
34:5	38:22
35:1–2	1:13
35:3	49:24–25; 117:7
35:7–10	81:5
35:10	133:27–33
40:3	45:71; 66:11; 33:10; 45:9; 65:1
40:4	84:28; 88:66
40:5	49:23; 133:22
40:6	101:23
40:31	124:7–8
42:7	89:20; 124:99
43:11	128:22
45:17	76:1; 35:25; 38:33
45:23	76:110; 88:104
49:1	1:1
49:2	6:2; 11:2; 12:2; 14:2; 15:2; 16:2; 33:1; 86:9
49:6	86:11
49:22	45:9, 115:5
50:2–3	35:8; 133:66–69
50:11	133:70
51:9–11	101:18
52:1	82:14; 113:7–8
52:2	113:9–10
52:7	19:29; 31:3; 113:10
52:8	39:13; 84:98–99
52:10	133:3
52:11	38:42; 133:5
52:12	49:27; 58:56; 101:68, 72; 133:15
52:15	101:94
54:2	82:14; 133:9
54:17	71:9; 109:25
55:6	88:62–63
59:17	27:15–18
60:1–4	64:41–42
60:2	112:23
60:22	133:58
61:1	128:22
62:4	133:23–24
62:10	45:9; 115:5
63:1–2	133:46–48
63:3–6	76:107; 88:106; 133:50–52
63:7–9	133:52–53
64:1–2	34:8; 133:40–42
64:3–5	76:10; 133:43–45
65:17	29:23
65:20	63:51; 101:30
65:21–22	101:101
66:1	38:17
66:24	76:44

Left: An oak of Bashan, near Qatzrin, an ancient village from the talmudic period (ca. A.D. 200–500). Bashan was a region north of Gilead and east of the Jordan River. The region was known to be fertile and was celebrated for its oak trees.

Below: A stand of cedars of Lebanon, east of Byblos. Mature cedars of Lebanon have large trunks and branches that spread out horizontally. In biblical times abundant forests of cedars flourished in the mountains of Lebanon, but now they are sparse.

Multiple ancient Near Eastern kingdoms imported cedars of Lebanon to use in many of their fine buildings. Hiram, king of Tyre, through an agreement with King Solomon, transported cedars to Jerusalem for Solomon's temple. Kings David and Solomon each used cedar in the construction of their personal residences.

ISAIAH 2:12–13

For the day of the Lord of hosts shall be upon every one that is proud and lofty, and upon every one that is lifted up; and he shall be brought low: And upon all the cedars of Lebanon, that are high and lifted up, and upon all the oaks of Bashan.

The phrase "day of the Lord" usually refers to the events connected with Jesus' second coming (2 Nephi 12:12–13; 23:6, 9). The day of the Lord is mentioned five times in Isaiah 2 to emphasize the event's importance. Throughout Isaiah, the phrases "day of the Lord," "in that day," "day of visitation," "day of his fierce anger," and "day of the Lord's vengeance" are found more than fifty-five times. This underscores how frequently Isaiah's writings emphasize the last days and the second coming.

Isaiah speaks of the Lord coming upon the cedars of Lebanon and oaks of Bashan in the last days. Bashan is a region east of the Jordan River and north of ancient Gilead. Lebanon is the nation immediately north of Israel known for its fine cedars. The scriptures consistently use trees to represent people (Psalm 1:3; 3 Nephi 14:17–18; D&C 135:6). In the context of Isaiah 2:11–21, oaks and cedars are like proud people, who, Isaiah informs his readers, are "high and lifted up." The day of the Lord will come and destroy them.

Above: Northwest tower of the Ajloun Castle, Jordan, built by Azz Al Din Au-sama in A.D. 1184–85. Large complex towers made of stone were built into the walls of fortified cities. Watchmen and guards stood on these towers, ready to warn the city's inhabitants of danger.

ISAIAH 2:13, 15

Yea, and the day of the Lord shall come . . . upon every high tower, and upon every fenced wall.

Towers and fences sometimes represent humanity's attempts to create protection from enemies and danger (Judges 9:46–52; Hosea 8:14). They are a demonstration of self-reliance. By contrast, the righteous rely on God for protection because for them God is a "wall of fire" (Zechariah 2:5) and a "high tower" that cannot be destroyed (2 Samuel 22:3; Psalm 18:2; 144:2). At the second coming, the Lord will destroy all man-made defenses, including towers and fenced walls. The safety they offer is temporary and unsure, but the protection the Lord offers is eternal and sure.

Left: Throughout the ages, the walls and fortresses of Jerusalem have been built, destroyed, and sometimes rebuilt. The stones reflect the culture and time of those who placed them. The remains of this wall date back to Isaiah's time.

ISAIAH 2:20

In that day a man shall cast his idols of silver, and his idols of gold, which they made each one for himself to worship, to the moles and to the bats.

When Jesus Christ comes in power, glory, and judgment upon the earth, the wicked will cast away their idols to the moles and bats. Seeing the Lord's glory, the wicked will be ashamed of their slavish dependence on any kind of false deity, including money, lust, or power.

Moles and bats dwell in darkness in holes and caves. According to the law of Moses, bats were not fit for human consumption: "They shall not be eaten, they are an abomination" (Leviticus 11:13, 19). Throwing idols to moles and bats may symbolize destroying idols or hiding them in dark places where they will not be seen.

ISAIAH 10:17

And the light of Israel shall be for a fire, and his Holy One for a flame: and it shall burn and devour his thorns and his briers in one day.

Isaiah 10:16–18 describes the destruction by fire of the forests and trees when Jesus comes. The trees represent people, specifically the people of ancient Assyria and the wicked of the last days. The Lord will put an end to their evil. The forest-fire imagery parallels the section of Isaiah in which God, as the forester, cuts down the forest of Assyria with his mighty ax (vv. 33–34).

Isaiah uses the parallel terms "thorns" and "briers" frequently (Isaiah 5:6; 7:23–25; 9:18; 27:4). He identifies the wicked as thorns and briers, meaning prickly, often dry plants that torment and afflict both man and beast. The wicked, at the coming of the Lord in power and glory, will be consumed as easily as the quick burning thorns and briers.

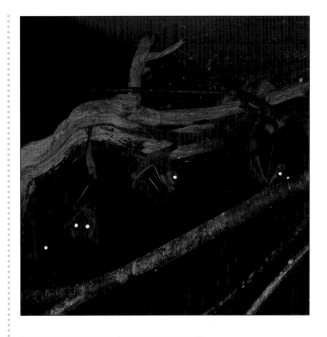

Above: Bats hanging from tree branches in a centuries-old building, Akko. Several species of bats live in the Near East, most of which eat insects. They dwell communally in caves, crevices, or other dark places.

Right: Thorns near Bethel. Thorns are prickly and fruitless plants that exist in the dry countryside of the Holy Land. The Bible mentions the vexatious nature of thorns (Genesis 3:18; Numbers 33:55; Joshua 23:13). Thorns are valuable only as quick burning fuel. Hence Isaiah's prophecy that the wicked, at Jesus' second coming, would burn as easily as thorns are consumed.

Buildings and Structures

altar(s)	6:6; 19:19
cottage	1:8
court(s)	34:13; 62:9
fort	29:3
fortress(es)	17:3; 25:12
foundation(s)	28:16; 44:28
gates	3:26; 13:2
habitation(s)	22:16; 27:10
house	2:3; 3:14
housetops	22:1; 37:27
lodge	1:8
monuments	65:4
palace(s)	25:2; 39:7
pillars	19:19
prison	42:7; 61:1
sanctuary	8:14; 16:12
tabernacle	4:6; 16:5
tower	2:15; 5:2
windows	24:18; 54:12

Weights and Measures

acre(s)	5:10
balance	40:12
bath	5:10
ephah	5:10; 60:6
flagons	22:24
homer	5:10
scales	40:12
span	40:12

ISAIAH 24:20

The earth shall reel to and fro like a drunkard, and shall be removed like a cottage; and the transgression thereof shall be heavy upon it; and it shall fall, and not rise again.

Isaiah's expression is poetic. He portrays the earth staggering about like a person whose sense of balance has been affected by strong drink. He also compares the movement of the earth to a man-made cottage.

The Lord says through Joseph Smith that the "earth groans under the weight of its iniquity" (D&C 123:7). Isaiah teaches that "the earth mourneth" (Isaiah 33:9). Moses records that when "Enoch heard the earth mourn, he wept, and cried unto the Lord, saying: O Lord, wilt thou not have compassion upon the earth?" (Moses 7:49).

In Isaiah 24:18–20, the prophet makes seven statements portraying the earth's reaction to the transgressions of humanity that are "heavy upon it": "the foundations of the earth do shake," "the earth is utterly broken down," "the earth is clean dissolved," "the earth is moved exceedingly," "the earth shall reel to and fro like a drunkard," the earth "shall be removed like a cottage," and the earth "shall fall, and not rise again." These expressions refer to great earthquakes that will occur in the last days when God's judgments come upon a wicked world (D&C 88:89). They may particularly refer to the last great earthquake that will occur at the time of the coming of the Lord (Revelation 16:18–20).

Right: Many cottages and huts from the biblical era were constructed of stones, like this cottage behind an olive tree, near Samaria. Cottages and huts often lack foundations, headers above windows and doorways, or proper support for the walls or roof. Isaiah may have had these unstable structures in mind when he compared the quaking earth to a cottage.

ISAIAH 30:27–28

Behold, the name of the Lord cometh from far, burning with his anger, and the burden thereof is heavy: his lips are full of indignation, and his tongue as a devouring fire: And his breath, as an overflowing stream, shall reach to the midst of the neck, to sift the nations with the sieve of vanity.

Isaiah 30:27–33 describes the destruction of the wicked that will take place at Jesus Christ's second coming, when the Lord comes from the distant heavens to cleanse the earth. Isaiah uses a number of descriptive phrases to describe the Lord's manner of punishing and destroying the wicked—"burning," "devouring fire," "flame of a devouring fire," "scattering," "tempest," "hailstones," and "brimstone."

In verse 28, Isaiah speaks of the "sieve of vanity," better translated as "the sieve of destruction." In the last days the Lord will sift the nations, removing the tares from the wheat with this sieve. In other words, he will separate the wicked from the righteous. In Amos 9:9, God uses the same "sieve" to "sift the house of Israel . . . , yet shall not the least grain fall upon the earth."

Isaiah assures those who dwell in Zion, the pure in heart who become one with their fellows, that they will be protected. He promises that they will sing songs to the Lord, worship at his temple, and experience a gladness of heart.

Who Will Dwell in the Celestial Kingdom?

Isaiah 33:14–17 pertains to the righteous dwelling in the celestial kingdom. The section begins with two parallel rhetorical questions asking who can dwell with God in his fire. Joseph Smith taught that "everlasting burnings" describes where God dwells (*Teachings of the Prophet Joseph Smith*, 361, 367). The two questions are followed by a response, detailing the attributes of one who is able to dwell with God. The response is followed by a promise of blessing to the righteous.

Questions

Who among us shall dwell with the devouring fire?
Who among us shall dwell with everlasting burnings?

Response

He that walketh righteously,
and speaketh uprightly;
he that despiseth the gain of oppressions,
that shaketh his hands from holding of bribes,
that stoppeth his ears from hearing of blood,
and shutteth his eyes from seeing evil.

Promise of Blessing

He shall dwell on high:
his place of defence shall be the munitions of rocks:
bread shall be given him; his waters shall be sure.
Thine eyes shall see the king in his beauty:
they shall behold the land that is very far off.

The Lord Promises the Resurrection

The Lord, through Isaiah, teaches about the resurrection. The words "live," "arise," "awake," and "sing" provide great comfort to those who anticipate the resurrection.

Isaiah 26:19

Thy dead men shall live,
together with my dead body shall they arise.
Awake and sing,
ye that dwell in dust: for thy dew is as the dew of herbs,
and the earth shall cast out the dead.

Left: Sieve, Neot Kedumim, a biblical landscape reserve. The pictured sieve is an instrument used to separate chaff or other debris from grain.

Peoples and Nationalities

Arabian	13:20
Assyrian	10:5, 24
Chaldeans	23:13; 43:14
Cush	11:11
Egyptians	19:2, 4
Elam	11:11
Ephraim	9:9
Gentiles	11:10; 42:1
Hamath	11:11
Israel	9:8
Javan	66:19
Judah	9:21
Levites	66:21
Manasseh	9:21
Medes	13:17
Pathros	11:11
Philistines	9:12; 11:14
Sabeans	45:14
Shinar	11:11
Syrians	9:12

Geographical Terms

bank(s)	8:7; 37:33
clifts	57:5
country/(tries)	1:7; 13:5
desert(s)	13:21; 48:21
earth	1:2; 2:19
field(s)	5:8; 7:3
flood	28:2; 59:19
hill(s)	5:1; 10:32
isle(s)	20:6; 23:2
land	1:7; 37:11
mount/mountain(s)	2:2; 8:18
pool(s)	7:3; 22:9
river(s)	7:20; 8:7
rock(s)	2:10; 8:14
sea	5:30; 17:12
spring(s)	42:9; 43:19
stone(s)	5:2; 9:10
stream(s)	27:12; 30:28
valley(s)	7:19; 22:7
water(s)	1:22; 8:6

ISAIAH 33:12

*And the people shall be as the burnings of lime:
as thorns cut up shall they be burned in the fire.*

Isaiah presents two images that deal with burning: "burnings of lime" and "burned in the fire." The first expression may refer to extracting lime from bones, a process requiring intense heat. (See Amos 2:1 for an example of burning bones.) Thus it would symbolize the complete destruction of the wicked at the Lord's coming. The second image pertains to thorns and weeds that are burned to prevent them from overcoming useful plants. When thorns are cut down and placed in a pile, they fuel a fire that becomes fierce and hot. Such will be the burning of the wicked at Christ's second coming.

Above: Briers, near Bethel. Briers, similar to thorns, are useful as fuel that burns quickly. On occasion briers are used to form natural fences.

The sword of the Lord is filled with blood, it is made fat with fatness, and with the blood of lambs and goats, with the fat of the kidneys of rams: for the Lord hath a sacrifice in Bozrah, and a great slaughter in the land of Idumea.

The language of Isaiah 34:1–8 uses symbolism from the Mosaic law of sacrifice. These verses suggest that the wicked will have to die for their own sins because they do not partake of the blessings of the sacrifice of Christ. The wicked will be slaughtered like the sacrificial animals in the temple (Jeremiah 46:10; Revelation 19:17–18). Bozrah (perhaps modern Busra) was the capital of Edom, here called Idumea. Idumea represents the wicked world (D&C 1:36) and will be destroyed by the Lord (Ezekiel 25:14).

Lambs, goats, and rams were sacrificial animals used for sin and trespass offerings to symbolically cleanse the repentant offerer from both willful and inadvertent sins. Under the Mosaic law of sacrifice, the blood and fat of a sacrificed animal are reserved for the Lord (Leviticus 3:15–17). By using the three words "blood," "fatness," and "kidneys" in the context of the slaughter of the wicked, Isaiah emphasizes the Lord's right to exact the penalty for iniquity. Blood and kidneys, with other internal organs, regulate the life of humans and beasts. The Lord's slaughter will be complete, claiming the very life force of the wicked.

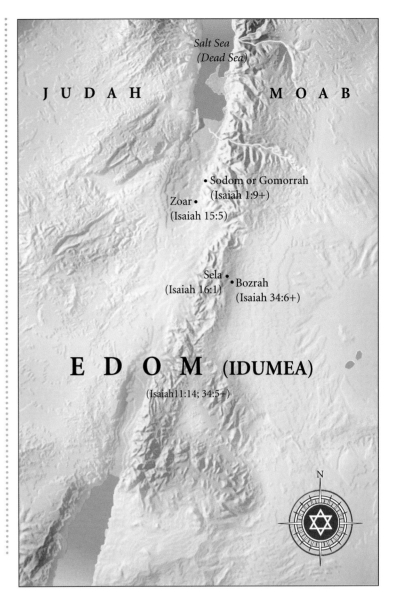

Edom at the Time of Isaiah

Left: A goat on a rock, Samaria. Goats played an important role in the temple and its regular sacrificial services (Leviticus 22:27). On the Day of Atonement, a goat was selected to become a scapegoat, one that would symbolically bear the sins of the Israelite nation (Leviticus 16:10–22).

Above: The sun sets on the Sea of Galilee. The Sea of Galilee is shaped like a harp. In Hebrew it is called *Kinneret,* the Hebrew word *kinnor* meaning "harp." The sea is approximately seven and one-half miles broad, twelve and one-half miles long, and is situated 680 feet below sea level. The Jordan River flows through the sea, north to south, and continues to the Dead Sea.

ISAIAH 60:20

Thy sun shall no more go down; neither shall thy moon withdraw itself: for the Lord shall be thine everlasting light.

Isaiah uses two heavenly spheres—the sun and the moon—to explain an eternal truth, that Jesus Christ is the everlasting light. In the millennial New Jerusalem, the Lord's light will be so consistent it will be as though both sun and moon are ever present. The Revelator describes a time similar to the one foretold by Isaiah, "And the city had no need of the sun, neither of the moon, to shine in it: for the glory of God did lighten it, and the Lamb is the light thereof" (Revelation 21:23). "And there shall be no night there; and they need no candle, neither light of the sun; for the Lord God giveth them light" (Revelation 22:5).

Isaiah Quotations and Paraphrases in the Book of Mormon

ISAIAH	BOOK OF MORMON

Direct Quotations

ISAIAH	BOOK OF MORMON
Isaiah 2–14	2 Nephi 12–24
Isaiah 48–49	1 Nephi 20–21
Isaiah 52:8–10	3 Nephi 16:18–20
Isaiah 52:15	3 Nephi 21:8
Isaiah 53	Mosiah 14:1–12
Isaiah 54	3 Nephi 22:1–17

Paraphrases

ISAIAH	BOOK OF MORMON
Isaiah 9:12–13	2 Nephi 28:32
Isaiah 11:4–9	2 Nephi 30:9, 12–15
Isaiah 11:11; 29:14	2 Nephi 25:11; 25:17; 29:1
Isaiah 28:10, 13	2 Nephi 28:30
Isaiah 29:3–5	2 Nephi 26:15–16, 18
Isaiah 29:4, 11	2 Nephi 27:6–9
Isaiah 29:6	2 Nephi 6:15
Isaiah 29:6–10	2 Nephi 27:2–5
Isaiah 29:13, 15	2 Nephi 28:9
Isaiah 29:13–24	2 Nephi 27:25–35
Isaiah 29:14	1 Nephi 14:7
Isaiah 29:21	2 Nephi 28:16
Isaiah 40:3	1 Nephi 10:8
Isaiah 45:18	1 Nephi 17:36
Isaiah 49:22	1 Nephi 22:6
Isaiah 49:22–23	1 Nephi 22:8
Isaiah 49:22–26	2 Nephi 6:6–7, 16–18
Isaiah 49:24–52:2	2 Nephi 6:16–8:25
Isaiah 52:1; 54:2	Moroni 10:31
Isaiah 52:1–3, 6–7, 11–15	3 Nephi 20:36–46
Isaiah 52:7	Mosiah 15:14–18
Isaiah 52:7	1 Nephi 13:47
Isaiah 52:7–10	Mosiah 12:21–24
Isaiah 52:8–10	Mosiah 15:29–31, 3 Nephi 20:32–35
Isaiah 52:10	1 Nephi 22:10–11
Isaiah 52:12	3 Nephi 21:29
Isaiah 53:10	Mosiah 15:10
Isaiah 55:1	2 Nephi 26:25
Isaiah 55:1–2	2 Nephi 9:50–51

Adapted from Donald W. Parry, Jay A. Parry, and Tina M. Peterson, *Understanding Isaiah,* 597–98.

The Great Isaiah Scroll, discovered in 1947, is one of the Dead Sea Scrolls.
The scroll contains all sixty-six chapters of Isaiah. It consists of seventeen pieces of animal skin sewn together to form a single scroll measuring twenty-four and one-half feet in length.

Types of Prophecy in the Book of Isaiah

Single Fulfillment

The assignment of one fulfillment to a prophecy. For example, Isaiah 53.

Multiple Fulfillment

More than one fulfillment to a prophecy. For example, Isaiah 2:1–3.

Conditional

The prophecy is not unconditional or absolute, but is based on one or more conditions. For example, Isaiah 1:19–20.

Unconditional

The prophecy is absolute, and no conditions are attached to it. For example, Isaiah 63:1–4.

Symbolic Action

The prophecy is communicated through nonverbal means. For example, Isaiah 20.

Type

A prophetic symbol that finds fulfillment in one or more later historic events. For example, Isaiah 8:18.

Right: Christ in a Red Robe, Minerva Teichert (1888–1976). Oil on canvas, 71¾" x 47¾", 1945.

ISAIAH 63:1–3

Who is this that cometh from Edom, with dyed garments from Bozrah? this that is glorious in his apparel, travelling in the greatness of his strength? I that speak in righteousness, mighty to save. Wherefore art thou red in thine apparel, and thy garments like him that treadeth in the winefat? I have trodden the winepress alone; and of the people there was none with me: for I will tread them in mine anger, and trample them in my fury; and their blood shall be sprinkled upon my garments, and I will stain all my raiment.

The opening verses of Isaiah 63 give two important questions and answers about the second coming of Christ. The first question is, Who comes with dyed garments traveling in the greatness of his strength? The answer: the Righteous One, who is mighty to save. The second question is, Why are your garments red, as one who has been treading in the winefat? The answer: because I have trodden the winepress alone, and I will trample the wicked and stain my garments with their blood.

When Christ returns, his garments will be red, as John saw: "And he was clothed with a vesture dipped in blood" (Revelation 19:13; D&C 133:48). The red clothing symbolizes at least two things: the blood Christ shed in accomplishing the atonement (Luke 22:44; D&C 19:18) and the blood of the unrepentant wicked he has slain in his wrath (Isaiah 63:3; Lamentations 1:15; D&C 133:48, 50–51). The blood symbolism is implied in the phrases "dyed garments," "garments like him . . . in the winefat," "winepress," "blood . . . upon my garments," and "stain all my raiment."

When Christ offered the atonement in the Garden of Gethsemane, his agony was so great that "his sweat was as it were great drops of blood" (Luke 22:44). This blood presumably stained his garments. In addition, the blood of the sins of all mankind—the signs of wickedness—will stain his garments. This blood of atonement is symbolized by the image of a man who treads red grapes in a winepress, staining his clothing with the juice. But, with Christ, not only his hem but his whole garment will be stained. His whole being was engaged in the work of atonement. He trod the winepress alone because only he could and did perform the atonement, kneeling in the Garden of Gethsemane and hanging on the cross. "I . . . have trodden the winepress alone, even the winepress of the fierceness of the wrath of Almighty God" (D&C 76:107; 88:106).

ILLUSTRATION CREDITS

Maps were created by Andrew Livingston.

Jacket
Isaiah, illustration by Gustave Doré
Sunset, pots, valley and flowers, olive tree,
    photographs by Carrilyn Clarkson
Falls, grapes, ship, photographs by Arnold
    H. Green
Gates, stone, lambs, photographs by Tana
    and Mac Graham
Laver, photograph by Andy North
Tomb, photograph by Justin Craig
Donald W. Parry, photograph by Bradley
    Slade
Acacia, photograph by D. Kelly Ogden

Frontispiece
Photograph by Carrilyn Clarkson

Page v
Camels, photograph by Arnold H. Green
Spring, acacia tree, fish, plow, photo-
    graphs by Tana and Mac Graham

Page vi
Photograph by Carrilyn Clarkson

Page ix
Photograph by Arnold H. Green

Page x
Photograph by Carrilyn Clarkson

Pages xii–1
Photograph by Carrilyn Clarkson

Page 3
Illustration by Gustave Doré

Page 4
Trough, ox, asses, photographs by Tana
    and Mac Graham

Page 5
Huts, photographs by Tana and Mac
    Graham

Page 6
Cistern at Jabal Sabir, photograph by
    Arnold H. Green
Grain, photograph by Brent Hall

Page 7
Cistern at Gibeon, grain storage, photo-
    graphs by Tana and Mac Graham

Page 8
Vineyard, winepress, photographs by Tana
    and Mac Graham

Page 9
Photograph by Arnold H. Green

Page 10
Photograph by *Biblical Archaeological
    Review* Mesop 4-085 © Erich
    Lessing/Art Resource, N.Y.

Page 11
Sycomore, photograph by Arnold H.
    Green
Bricks, photograph by Tana and Mac
    Graham

Page 12
Photograph © by Hershel Shanks

From top: Poppies near the valley of Elah, the Mediterranean seashore in Caesarea, olive tree in the Garden of Gethsemane, the mountainside by Gamla, the Salt Lake Temple.

Page 14
Natural chalk, beaten chalk stone, photographs by Tana and Mac Graham

Page 15
Photograph by Tana and Mac Graham

Page 16
Photograph by Tana and Mac Graham

Page 17
Broken pottery, cow, photographs by Tana and Mac Graham

Page 18
Photograph by Carrilyn Clarkson

Page 19
Temples, photographs by Andy North

Page 20
Dovecote, loom, photographs by Tana and Mac Graham

Page 21
Photograph by Carrilyn Clarkson

Page 22
Photograph by Justin Craig

Page 23
Wildlife, horse, photographs by Tana and Mac Graham

Pages 24–25
Photograph by Carrilyn Clarkson

Page 26
Ship, bees, razor, photographs by Tana and Mac Graham

Page 27
Photograph by Arnold H. Green

Page 29
Photograph by Tana and Mac Graham

Page 81

Photograph by Carrilyn Clarkson

Page 82

Herodian cornerstones, early cornerstones, photographs by Tana and Mac Graham

Page 84

Plow, plowman and ass, photographs by Tana and Mac Graham

Page 85

Thicket, shepherd, photographs by Tana and Mac Graham

Page 86

Photograph by Tana and Mac Graham

Page 87

Old man, photograph by Tana and Mac Graham

Clouds, photograph by Carrilyn Clarkson

Page 88

Wall close-up, photograph by Brent Hall

Gate, "Golden Gate in Jerusalem" © Zev Radovan

Page 89

Photograph by Tana and Mac Graham

Page 90

"The ankle bone of a crucified man." © Zev Radovan

Page 91

Red olive oil, photograph by Matthew J. Grey

Olive press, photograph by Tana and Mac Graham

Page 92

Photograph by Carrilyn Clarkson

Page 93

Photograph by Tana and Mac Graham

Page 94

Garden Tomb © Richard Nowitz

River, photograph by Arnold H. Green

Page 95

Clay pots, potter, photographs by Carrilyn Clarkson

Pages 96–97

Photograph by Arnold H. Green

Page 99

Photograph "Temple Reflections" © 2000 by Leigh Gunnell

Page 101

Waves, photograph by Tana and Mac Graham

Sand dunes, photograph by D. Kelly Ogden

Page 102

Leopard, goats, photographs by Tana and Mac Graham

Boy, photograph by Carrilyn Clarkson

Page 103

Photograph by D. Kelly Odgen

Page 104

Idols, white blossoms, almond blossoms, photographs by Tana and Mac Graham

Page 105

Photograph by Carrilyn Clarkson

Page 106

Reeds, photograph by Carrilyn Clarkson

Parched earth, photograph by Tana and Mac Graham

SOURCES CONSULTED

Achtemeier, Paul J., ed. *The Harper Collins Bible Dictionary*. Rev. ed. San Francisco: Harper, 1996.

Butler, Trent C., ed. *Holman Bible Dictionary*. Nashville, Tenn.: Holman Bible Publishers, 1991.

Dockery, David S., ed. *Holman Bible Handbook*. Nashville, Tenn.: Holman Bible Publishers, 1992.

Douglas, J. D., et al., eds. *The Illustrated Bible Dictionary*. Downers Grove, Ill.: Inter-Varsity Press, 1998.

——, eds. *New Bible Dictionary*. 2d ed. Wheaton, Ill.: Tyndale House Publishers, 1982.

Elwell, Walter A., ed. *Baker Encyclopedia of the Bible*. Vol. 1 Grand Rapids, Mich.: Baker Books, 1988.

Freedman, David Noel, ed. *The Anchor Bible Dictionary*. New York: Doubleday, 1992.

——, ed. *Eerdmans Dictionary of the Bible*. Grand Rapids, Mich.: Eerdmans, 2000.

Freeman, James M. *Manners and Customs of the Bible*. Plainfield, N.J.: Logos, 1972.

Gower, Ralph. *The New Manners and Customs of Bible Times*. Chicago: Moody Press, 1987.

Grosvenor, Melville Bell, ed. *Everyday Life in Bible Times*. Washington, D.C.: National Geographic Society, 1967.

Hepper, F. Nigel. *Baker Encyclopedia of Bible Plants*. Grand Rapids, Mich.: Baker, 1992.

Matthews, Victor H. *Manners and Customs in the Bible*. Peabody, Mass.: Hendrickson, 1991.

Parry, Donald W. *Harmonizing Isaiah: Combining Ancient Sources*. Provo, Utah: FARMS, 2001.

Parry, Donald W., Jay A. Parry, Tina M. Peterson. *Understanding Isaiah*. Salt Lake City, Utah: Deseret Book, 1998.

Parry, Donald W., and John W. Welch. *Isaiah in the Book of Mormon*. Provo, Utah: FARMS, 1998.

Pritchard, James B., ed. *Ancient Near Eastern Texts: Relating to the Old Testament*. 3d ed. with supplement. Princeton, N.J.: Princeton University Press, 1969.

Rogerson, John. *Chronicle of the Old Testament Kings*. London: Thames and Hudson, 1999.

Smith, Joseph. *History of the Church of Jesus Christ of Latter-day Saints*. Edited by B. H. Roberts. 2d ed. Salt Lake City, Utah: Church of Jesus Christ of Latter-day Saints, 1980.

——. *Joseph Smith's Commentary on the Bible*. Compiled and edited by Kent P. Jackson. Salt Lake City, Utah: Deseret Book, 1994.

——. *Teachings of the Prophet Joseph Smith*. Selected by Joseph Fielding Smith. Salt Lake City, Utah: Deseret Book, 1976.

Unger, Merrill F. *Unger's Bible Dictionary*. Chicago: Moody Press, 1981.

SCRIPTURE INDEX